D1048444

FIRST NAME

HOME ADDRESS (LINE 1)

HOME ADDRESS (LINE 2)

HOME PHONE   MOBILE PHONE

EMAIL

TWITTER   INSTAGRAM

BUSINESS/COLLEGE ADDRESS (LINE 1)

BUSINESS/COLLEGE ADDRESS (LINE 2)

BUSINESS/COLLEGE PHONE   BUSINESS/COLLEGE EMAIL

EMERGENCY CONTACT (NAME AND PHONE NUMBER)

BLOOD GROUP

ALLERGIES

VACCINATIONS

UK BANK HOLIDAYS

JANUARY 1ST — New Year's Day

APRIL 2ND — Good Friday

APRIL 5TH — Easter Monday

MAY 3RD — Early May Bank Holiday

MAY 31ST — Spring Bank Holiday

AUGUST 30TH — Summer Bank Holiday

DECEMBER 27TH — Substitute for Christmas Day

DECEMBER 28TH — Substitute for Boxing Day Holiday

US FEDERAL HOLIDAYS

JANUARY 1ST — New Year's Day

JANUARY 18TH — Martin Luther King Day

FEBRUARY 15TH — Presidents' Day

MAY 31ST — Memorial Day

JULY 5TH — Independence Day (observed)

SEPTEMBER 6TH — Labor Day

OCTOBER 11TH — Indigenous Peoples' Day

NOVEMBER 11TH — Veterans Day

NOVEMBER 25TH — Thanksgiving

DECEMBER 24TH — Substitute for Christmas Day

Verso Books is the largest independent,
radical publishing house in the English-speaking world.

Launched by *New Left Review* in 1970, Verso
is a leading publisher in current affairs, philosophy,
history, politics and economics.

"A rigorously intelligent publisher."
—*SUNDAY TIMES*

"Anglo-America's preeminent radical press."
—*HARPER'S*

VERSOBOOKS.COM

Buy securely and easily from our website—
great discounts, free shipping with a minimum order
and a free ebook bundled with many of our hard-copy books.

Check our website to read our blog and see our
latest titles—featuring essays, videos, podcasts,
interviews with authors, news, exclusive competitions
and details of forthcoming events.

Sign up to our email list to be the first to hear of
our new titles, special offers and events.

Verso Books   @VersoBooks   versobooks

Some of the quotes in the calendar are drawn
from *The Verso Book of Dissent*, edited by
Andrew Hsiao and Audrea Lim (Verso 2020).

2021

JANUARY

S	M	T	W	TH	F	S
27	28	29	30	31	1	2
3	4	5	6	7	8	9
10	11	12	13	14	15	16
17	18	19	20	21	22	23
24	25	26	27	28	29	30
31						

FEBRUARY

S	M	T	W	TH	F	S
31	1	2	3	4	5	6
7	8	9	10	11	12	13
14	15	16	17	18	19	20
21	22	23	24	25	26	27
28	1	2	3	4	5	6

MARCH

S	M	T	W	TH	F	S
28	1	2	3	4	5	6
7	8	9	10	11	12	13
14	15	16	17	18	19	20
21	22	23	24	25	26	27
28	29	30	31	1	2	3

APRIL

S	M	T	W	TH	F	S
28	29	30	31	1	2	3
4	5	6	7	8	9	10
11	12	13	14	15	16	17
18	19	20	21	22	23	24
25	26	27	28	29	30	1

MAY

S	M	T	W	TH	F	S
25	26	27	28	29	30	1
2	3	4	5	6	7	8
9	10	11	12	13	14	15
16	17	18	19	20	21	22
23	24	25	26	27	28	29
30	31					

JUNE

S	M	T	W	TH	F	S
30	31	1	2	3	4	5
6	7	8	9	10	11	12
13	14	15	16	17	18	19
20	21	22	23	24	25	26
27	28	29	30	1	2	3

JULY

S	M	T	W	TH	F	S
27	28	29	30	1	2	3
4	5	6	7	8	9	10
11	12	13	14	15	16	17
18	19	20	21	22	23	24
25	26	27	28	29	30	31

AUGUST

S	M	T	W	TH	F	S
1	2	3	4	5	6	7
8	9	10	11	12	13	14
15	16	17	18	19	20	21
22	23	24	25	26	27	28
29	30	31	1	2	3	4

SEPTEMBER

S	M	T	W	TH	F	S
28	29	31	1	2	3	4
5	6	7	8	9	10	11
12	13	14	15	16	17	18
19	20	21	22	23	24	25
26	27	28	29	30	1	2

OCTOBER

S	M	T	W	TH	F	S
26	27	28	29	30	1	2
3	4	5	6	7	8	9
10	11	12	13	14	15	16
17	18	19	20	21	22	23
24	25	26	27	28	29	30
31						

NOVEMBER

S	M	T	W	TH	F	S
31	1	2	3	4	5	6
7	8	9	10	11	12	13
14	15	16	17	18	19	20
21	22	23	24	25	26	27
28	29	30	1	2	3	4

DECEMBER

S	M	T	W	TH	F	S
28	29	30	1	2	3	4
5	6	7	8	9	10	11
12	13	14	15	16	17	18
19	20	21	22	23	24	25
26	27	28	29	30	31	1

2022

JANUARY

S	M	T	W	TH	F	S
26	27	28	29	30	31	1
2	3	4	5	6	7	8
9	10	11	12	13	14	15
16	17	18	19	20	21	22
23	24	25	26	27	28	29
30	31					

FEBRUARY

S	M	T	W	TH	F	S
30	31	1	2	3	4	5
6	7	8	9	10	11	12
13	14	15	16	17	18	19
20	21	22	23	24	25	26
27	28	1	2	3	4	5

MARCH

S	M	T	W	TH	F	S
27	28	1	2	3	4	5
6	7	8	9	10	11	12
13	14	15	16	17	18	19
20	21	22	23	24	25	26
27	28	29	30	31	1	2

APRIL

S	M	T	W	TH	F	S
27	28	29	30	31	1	2
3	4	5	6	7	8	9
10	11	12	13	14	15	16
17	18	19	20	21	22	23
24	25	26	27	28	29	30

MAY

S	M	T	W	TH	F	S
1	2	3	4	5	6	7
8	9	10	11	12	13	14
15	16	17	18	19	20	21
22	23	24	25	26	27	28
29	30	31	1	2	3	4

JUNE

S	M	T	W	TH	F	S
29	30	31	1	2	3	4
5	6	7	8	9	10	11
12	13	14	15	16	17	18
19	20	21	22	23	24	25
26	27	28	29	30	1	2

JULY

S	M	T	W	TH	F	S
26	27	28	29	30	1	2
3	4	5	6	7	8	9
10	11	12	13	14	15	16
17	18	19	20	21	22	23
24	25	26	27	28	29	30
31						

AUGUST

S	M	T	W	TH	F	S
31	1	2	3	4	5	6
7	8	9	10	11	12	13
14	15	16	17	18	19	20
21	22	23	24	25	26	27
28	29	30	31			

SEPTEMBER

S	M	T	W	TH	F	S
28	29	30	31	1	2	3
4	5	6	7	8	9	10
11	12	13	14	15	16	17
18	19	20	21	22	23	24
25	26	27	28	29	30	1

OCTOBER

S	M	T	W	TH	F	S
25	26	27	28	29	30	1
2	3	4	5	6	7	8
9	10	11	12	13	14	15
16	17	18	19	20	21	22
23	24	25	26	27	28	29
30	31					

NOVEMBER

S	M	T	W	TH	F	S
30	31	1	2	3	4	5
6	7	8	9	10	11	12
13	14	15	16	17	18	19
20	21	22	23	24	25	26
27	28	29	30	1	2	3

DECEMBER

S	M	T	W	TH	F	S
27	28	29	30	1	2	3
4	5	6	7	8	9	10
11	12	13	14	15	16	17
18	19	20	21	22	23	24
25	26	27	28	29	30	31

VERSO CLASSICS: A READING LIST

Verso—the left-hand page—has been publishing landmark radical books for over 50 years, by thinkers including Tariq Ali, Walter Benjamin, Ellen Meiksins Wood, Perry Anderson, Angela Davis, Judith Butler, Theodor Adorno, and many more. In this reading list we bring you a selection of books from across our publishing; a starting place for exploring 50 years of radical ideas.

VERSO BOOK OF DISSENT
ANDY HSIAO & AUDREA LIM

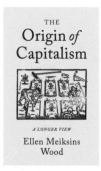

THE ORIGIN OF CAPITALISM
ELLEN MEIKSINS WOOD

THE FORCE OF NON VIOLENCE
JUDITH BUTLER

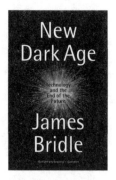

NEW DARK AGE
JAMES BRIDLE

50 YEARS OF VERSO BOOKS

I, RIGOBERTA MENCHÚ:
AN INDIAN WOMAN IN GUATEMALA
RIGOBERTA MENCHÚ

THE VERSO BOOK OF FEMINISM:
REVOLUTIONARY WORDS FROM FOUR
MILLENNIA OF REBELLION
EDITED BY JESSIE KINDIG

CONSIDERATIONS ON WESTERN MARXISM
PERRY ANDERSON

READING CAPITAL
LOUIS ALTHUSSER AND ETIENNE BALIBAR

POSTMODERNISM, OR,
THE CULTURAL LOGIC OF LATE CAPITALISM
FREDRIC JAMESON

MINIMA MORALIA:
REFLECTIONS FROM DAMAGED LIFE
THEODOR ADORNO

INVENTING THE FUTURE: POSTCAPITALISM
AND A WORLD WITHOUT WORK
NICK SRNICEK AND ALEX WILLIAMS

THE COMPLETE WORKS OF
ROSA LUXEMBURG, VOLUME I:
ECONOMIC WRITINGS 1
ROSA LUXEMBURG

THE SUBLIME OBJECT OF IDEOLOGY
SLAVOJ ŽIŽEK

IMAGINED COMMUNITIES
BENEDICT ANDERSON

CHAVS: THE DEMONIZATION OF THE
WORKING CLASS
OWEN JONES

IF THEY COME IN THE MORNING…:
VOICES OF RESISTANCE
EDITED BY ANGELA Y. DAVIS

CRITIQUE OF EVERYDAY LIFE:
THE ONE-VOLUME EDITION
HENRI LEFEBVRE

REVOLTING PROSTITUTES
JUNO MAC AND MOLLY SMITH

A PLANET TO WIN:
WHY WE NEED A GREEN NEW DEAL
KATE ARONOFF, ALYSSA BATTISTONI, ET AL.

AESTHETICS AND POLITICS
THEODOR ADORNO, WALTER BENJAMIN,
ET AL.

MISTAKEN IDENTITY:
RACE AND CLASS IN THE AGE OF TRUMP
ASAD HAIDER

RED ROSA: A GRAPHIC BIOGRAPHY
OF ROSA LUXEMBURG
KATE EVANS

ARTIFICIAL HELLS: PARTICIPATORY ART
AND THE POLITICS OF SPECTATORSHIP
CLAIRE BISHOP

THE LEFT HEMISPHERE:
MAPPING CRITICAL THEORY TODAY
RAZMIG KEUCHEYAN

FORTUNES OF FEMINISM:
FROM STATE-MANAGED CAPITALISM
TO NEOLIBERAL CRISIS
NANCY FRASER

PORTRAITS: JOHN BERGER ON ARTISTS
JOHN BERGER

PLANET OF SLUMS
MIKE DAVIS

OCTOBER: THE STORY OF
THE RUSSIAN REVOLUTION
CHINA MIÉVILLE

SUNDAY DECEMBER 27

JANUARY 1, 1994 Zapatista forces overtake towns in Chiapas, beginning an ongoing revolution against the Mexican state. "The dispossessed, we are millions, and we thereby call upon our brothers and sisters to join this struggle as the only path."
—ZAPATISTA ARMY OF NATIONAL LIBERATION

JANUARY 1, 2009 Oscar Grant III was a twenty-two-year-old black man, fatally shot by an Oakland, California, transit cop in the early morning hours of the New Year. The riots that followed were some of the largest the United States had seen in decades. "Oscar Grant: Murdered. The Whole Damn System Is Guilty!"
—PLACARD FROM THE OSCAR GRANT REBELLION

MONDAY DECEMBER 28

TUESDAY DECEMBER 29

WEDNESDAY DECEMBER 30

_____

_____

_____

_____

_____

_____

_____

Subcomandante Marcos and Comandante Tacho in La Realidad, Chiapas, 1999

THURSDAY DECEMBER 31

_____

_____

_____

_____

_____

_____

_____

NOTES:

_____

_____

_____

_____

_____

_____

FRIDAY JANUARY 01

_____

_____

_____

_____

_____

_____

_____

SATURDAY JANUARY 02

_____

_____

_____

_____

_____

_____

_____

SUNDAY JANUARY 03

MONDAY JANUARY 04

TUESDAY JANUARY 05

JANUARY 3, 1961 Angolan peasants employed by the Portuguese-Belgium cotton plantation company Cotonang begin protests over poor working conditions, setting off the Angolan struggle for independence from Portugal.

> "Tomorrow we will sing songs of freedom
> when we commemorate
> the day this slavery ends."
> —FIRST PRESIDENT OF ANGOLA AND LEADER OF
> THE MOVEMENT FOR THE LIBERATION OF ANGOLA
> ANTONIO AGOSTINHO NETO, "FAREWELL AT THE HOUR
> OF PARTING"

JANUARY 5, 1971 Angela Davis—black feminist, philosopher, and prison abolitionist—declares her innocence in a California court over the kidnapping and murder of a judge. "Prisons do not disappear problems, they disappear human beings. And the practice of disappearing vast numbers of people from poor, immigrant, and racially marginalized communities has literally become big business."
—"MASKED RACISM"

JANUARY 7, 1957 Djamila Bouhired, the "Arab Joan of Arc" and member of the National Liberation Front, sets off a bomb in an Algiers café, precipitating the Battle of Algiers, a pivotal episode in the Algerian struggle for independence against the French. "It was the most beautiful day of my life because I was confident that I was going to be dying for the sake of the most wonderful story in the world."

JANUARY 9, 1959 Rigoberta Menchú Tum, indigenous revolutionary and Nobel Peace Prize winner, is born in Chimel, Guatemala. "[My cause] wasn't born out of something good, it was born out of wretchedness and bitterness. It has been radicalized by the poverty in which my people live."
—I, RIGOBERTA MENCHÚ

WEDNESDAY JANUARY 06

_____

_____

_____

_____

_____

_____

_____

Rigoberta Menchú Tum, indigenous revolutionary and Nobel Peace Prize winner

THURSDAY JANUARY 07

_____

_____

_____

_____

_____

_____

_____

NOTES:

_____

_____

_____

_____

_____

_____

FRIDAY JANUARY 08

_____

_____

_____

_____

_____

_____

_____

SATURDAY JANUARY 09

_____

_____

_____

_____

_____

_____

SUNDAY JANUARY 10

_____

_____

_____

_____

_____

_____

_____

_____

MONDAY JANUARY 11

_____

_____

_____

_____

_____

_____

_____

TUESDAY JANUARY 12

_____

_____

_____

_____

_____

_____

_____

JANUARY 10, 1776 Thomas Paine, who participated in the American and French revolutions, publishes the pamphlet _Common Sense_, which argued for American independence from Britain. "Society in every state is a blessing, but government even in its best state is but a necessary evil; in its worst state an intolerable one."

JANUARY 11, 1894 Donghak Rebellion begins in Mujiang, Korea, over local corruption, eventually growing into an anti-establishment movement. "The people are the root of the nation. If the root withers, the nation will be enfeebled." —DONGHAK REBELLION PROCLAMATION

JANUARY 11, 1912 Workers in Lawrence, Massachusetts, walk out over a race-based pay cut in what would become known as the "bread and roses" strike. Soon an Industrial Workers of the World–organized strike shuts down every textile mill in the city.

JANUARY 13, 1898 Émile Zola publishes his infamous letter, "J'accuse ... !," accusing the French government of framing Jewish general Alfred Dreyfus for sabotage.

JANUARY 15, 1919 Rosa Luxemburg, founder of the Spartacus League, is murdered by the German Social Democratic government. "The madness will cease and the bloody demons of hell will vanish only when workers in Germany and France, England and Russia finally awake from their stupor, extend to each other a brotherly hand, and drown out the bestial chorus of imperialist war-mongers." —JUNIUS PAMPHLET

WEDNESDAY JANUARY 13

Strikers face the Massachusetts State Militia, 1912

THURSDAY JANUARY 14

NOTES:

FRIDAY JANUARY 15

SATURDAY JANUARY 16

SUNDAY JANUARY 17

MONDAY JANUARY 18

TUESDAY JANUARY 19

JANUARY 17, 1893 Queen Lili'uokalani, Hawaii's last monarch, is overthrown by American colonists.

JANUARY 17, 1961 Patrice Lumumba, Congolese independence leader and first prime minister of independent Congo, is assassinated by the Belgian government. Six months earlier, he had been deposed in a CIA-backed coup. "They are trying to distort your focus when they call our government a communist government, in the pay of the Soviet Union, or say that Lumumba is a communist, an anti-white: Lumumba is an African."

JANUARY 20, 1973 Amílcar Cabral, a communist intellectual and guerrilla leader of Guinea-Bissau's anti-colonial movement against the Portuguese, is assassinated. Guinea-Bissau became independent just months later. "Honesty, in a political context, is total commitment and total identification with the toiling masses."

JANUARY 20, 2017 Hundreds of protesters are arrested in Washington, DC as Donald Trump is inaugurated as US president, and the following day, an estimated 470,000 people rally for the Women's March on Washington. "Pussy Grabs Back." —PROTEST SLOGAN

JANUARY 23, 1976 Paul Robeson, the African-American singer and civil rights campaigner, dies. "I stand always on the side of those who will toil and labor. As an artist I come to sing, but as a citizen, I will always speak for peace, and no one can silence me in this."

WEDNESDAY JANUARY 20

Patrice Lumumba (1925–1961) raises his unshackled arms
following his release, 1960

THURSDAY JANUARY 21

NOTES:

FRIDAY JANUARY 22

SATURDAY JANUARY 23

A MOVEMENT HISTORY OF LOS ANGELES
MIKE DAVIS

In August 1965 thousands of young Black people in Watts set fire to the illusion that Los Angeles was a youth paradise. Since the debut of the TV show *77 Sunset Strip* in 1958, followed by the first of the Gidget romance films in 1959 and then the Beach Boys' "Surfin' USA" in 1963, teenagers in the rest of the country had become intoxicated with images of the endless summer that supposedly defined adolescence in Southern California. Edited out of utopia was the existence of a rapidly growing population

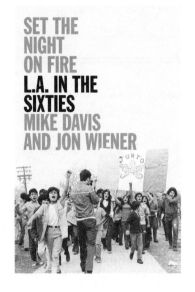

of more than 1 million people of African, Asian, and Mexican ancestry. Their kids were restricted to a handful of beaches; everywhere else, they risked arrest by local cops or beatings by white gangs. Economic opportunity was also rationed. During the first half of the Sixties, hundreds of brand-new college classrooms beckoned to white kids with an offer of free higher education, while factories and construction sites begged for more workers. But failing inner-city high schools with extreme dropout rates reduced the college admissions of Black and brown youth to a small trickle. Despite virtually full employment for whites, Black youth joblessness dramatically increased, as did the index of residential segregation.

L.A.'s streets and campuses in the Sixties also provided stages for many other groups to assert demands for free speech, equality, peace and justice. Initially these protests tended to be one-issue campaigns, but the grinding forces of repression—above all the Vietnam draft and the LAPD—drew them together in formal and informal alliances. LGBT activists coordinated actions with youth activists in protest of police and sheriffs' dragnets on Sunset Strip, in turn making "Free Huey" one of their demands. When Black and Chicano high school kids "blew out" their campuses in 1968–69, several thousand white students walked out in solidarity. A brutal LAPD attack on thousands of middle-class antiwar protesters at the Century Plaza Hotel in 1967 hastened the development of a biracial coalition supporting Tom Bradley, a liberal Black council member, in his crusade to wrest City Hall from right-wing populist Sam Yorty. In the same period the antiwar movement joined hands with the Black Panthers to form California's unique Peace and Freedom Party.

Periodization is often fraught for historians, who understand the necessity of temporal frameworks but also their artificiality. The Sixties in L.A., however, have obvious bookends. We start in 1960 because that year saw the appearance of social forces that would coalesce into the movements of the era, along with the emergence of a new agenda for social change, especially around what might be called the "issue of issues": racial segregation. In L.A. those developments overlapped with the beginning of the regime of Sam Yorty, elected mayor in 1961. 1973, on the other hand, marked not only the end of protest in the streets but also the defeat of Yorty and the advent of the efficient, pro-business administration of Tom Bradley.

There were also three important turning points that subdivide the long decade. 1963 was a roller-coaster year that witnessed the first: the rise and fall of the United Civil Rights Committee, the most important attempt to integrate housing, schools and jobs in L.A. through nonviolent protest and negotiation. 1965 saw the second turning point, the so-called Watts Riots. The third was in 1969, which began as a year of hope with a strong coalition of white liberals, Blacks and newly minted Chicanos supporting Bradley for mayor. He led the polls until election eve, when Yorty counterattacked with a vicious barrage of racist and red-baiting appeals to white voters. Bradley's defeat foreclosed, at least for the foreseeable future, any concessions to the city's minorities or liberal voters. Moreover, it was immediately followed by sinister campaigns, involving the FBI, the district attorney's office, and both the LAPD and L.A. County Sheriffs to destroy the Panthers, Brown Berets and other radical groups. This is the true context underlying the creeping sense of dread and imminent chaos famously evoked by Joan Didion in her 1979 essay collection, *The White Album*. If "helter skelter" was unleashed after 1970, the Manson gang were bit players compared to the institutions of law and order.

This is a revised extract from Set the Night on Fire: L.A. in the Sixties *by Mike Davis and Jon Wiener (Verso, 2020).*

SUNDAY JANUARY 24

MONDAY JANUARY 25

TUESDAY JANUARY 26

JANUARY 24, 1911 The anarcho-feminist Kanno Sugako is hanged for plotting to assassinate Emperor Meiji. "In accordance with long-standing customs, we have been seen as a form of material property. Women in Japan are in a state of slavery."
—"WOMEN ARE SLAVES"

JANUARY 27, 1924 Lenin's funeral takes place in Red Square. In attendance was the poet Vladimir Mayakovsky, who went on to pen the epic poem, "Vladimir Ilyich Lenin."

> "Just guzzling
> snoozing
> and pocketing pelf,
> Capitalism
> got lazy and feeble."

JANUARY 28, 1948 A plane crash kills twenty-eight bracero farm workers being sent back to Mexico. Cesar Chavez considered the moment part of his early political education.

> "Who are all these friends, all scattered like dry leaves?
> The radio says, 'They are just deportees ...'"
> —WOODY GUTHRIE, "DEPORTEE"

JANUARY 29, 1967 Arusha Declaration, written by Julius Nyerere, is issued to clarify Tanzania's path toward Ujamaa, or African socialism. "We, in Africa, have no more need of being 'converted' to socialism than we have of being 'taught' democracy."
—"UJAMAA, THE BASIS OF AFRICAN SOCIALISM"

JANUARY 30, 1972 British soldiers shot twenty-eight unarmed civilians in Northern Ireland during a peaceful protest march against internment, in what become known as Bloody Sunday—one of the most significant brutal events of The Troubles.

WEDNESDAY JANUARY 27

The 35th Bloody Sunday memorial march in Derry, 28 January 2007

THURSDAY JANUARY 28

NOTES:

FRIDAY JANUARY 29

SATURDAY JANUARY 30

SUNDAY JANUARY 31

MONDAY FEBRUARY 01

TUESDAY FEBRUARY 02

FEBRUARY 1, 1902 Langston Hughes, poet and figure of the Harlem Renaissance, is born.

"What happens to a dream deferred?
Does it dry up
like a raisin in the sun?
Or fester like a sore—
and then run?"
—"MONTAGE OF A DREAM DEFERRED"

FEBRUARY 2, 1512 Taíno hero Hatuey is captured and killed after besieging the Spaniards for four months at their first fort in Cuba. "[Gold] is the God the Spaniards worship. For these they fight and kill, for these they persecute us and that is why we have to throw them into the sea." —HATUEY'S SPEECH TO THE TAÍNOS

FEBRUARY 3, 1930 The Indochinese Communist Party is established; it conducted an underground struggle against the French colonialists and, later, the American invaders.

FEBRUARY 4, 1899 Philippine-American war begins after the Philippine government objects to being handed over to the US from Spain.

"The North
Americans have
captured nothing
but a vessel
of water,
nothing that
our sun
will find difficult
to empty with its rage."
—ALFREDO NAVARRO SALANGA

WEDNESDAY FEBRUARY 03

Torture of Hatuey in Cuba, by Theodor de Bry, 1590

THURSDAY FEBRUARY 04

NOTES:

FRIDAY FEBRUARY 05

SATURDAY FEBRUARY 06

SUNDAY FEBRUARY 07

FEBRUARY 7, 1948 Tens of thousands of silent marchers in Bogotá memorialize victims of Colombian state violence. "Señor Presidente, our flag is in mourning; this silent multitude, the mute cry from our hearts, asks only that you treat us … as you would have us treat you." —JORGE ELIÉCER GAITÁN, LEADER OF THE COLOMBIAN LIBERAL PARTY

FEBRUARY 8, 1677 Andrew Marvell, English poet and parliamentarian during the Anglo-Dutch wars, publishes his last known work. "There has now for divers years a design been carried on to change the lawful government of England into an absolute tyranny." —AN ACCOUNT OF THE GROWTH OF POPERY AND ARBITRARY GOVERNMENT IN ENGLAND

MONDAY FEBRUARY 08

FEBRUARY 8, 1996 John Perry Barlow publishes "A Declaration of the Independence of Cyberspace" in response to an anti-pornography bill passed by the US Congress that would have chilled online speech dramatically. "On behalf of the future, I ask you of the past to leave us alone."

FEBRUARY 10, 1883 The Russian revolutionary Vera Figner is arrested for her role in Tsar Alexander II's assassination. She received a death sentence that was later commuted. "My past experience had convinced me that the only way to change the existing order was by force." —MEMOIRS OF A REVOLUTIONIST

TUESDAY FEBRUARY 09

FEBRUARY 11, 1916 Emma Goldman, anarchist agitator, publisher and all-around "rebel woman," is arrested for distributing a pamphlet about birth control written by Margaret Sanger.

FEBRUARY 11, 1990 Nelson Mandela is freed after twenty-seven years as a political prisoner. Four years later he became the first president of post-apartheid South Africa.

WEDNESDAY FEBRUARY 10

Vera Nikolayevna Figner (1852–1942) after the 1905 Russian Revolution

THURSDAY FEBRUARY 11

NOTES:

FRIDAY FEBRUARY 12

SATURDAY FEBRUARY 13

SUNDAY FEBRUARY 14

_____

_____

_____

_____

_____

_____

_____

_____

MONDAY FEBRUARY 15

_____

_____

_____

_____

_____

_____

_____

TUESDAY FEBRUARY 16

_____

_____

_____

_____

_____

_____

_____

FEBRUARY 14, 1818 The birth date chosen by Frederick Douglass, America's foremost abolitionist writer and activist. "What, to the American slave, is your 4th of July? I answer: a day that reveals to him, more than all other days in the year, the gross injustice and cruelty to which he is the constant victim." —"THE MEANING OF JULY FOURTH FOR THE NEGRO"

FEBRUARY 15, 1855 Muktabai, a fourteen-year-old Dalit, publishes the earliest surviving piece of writing by an "untouchable" woman. "Let that religion, where only one person is privileged and the rest are deprived, perish from the earth and let it never enter our minds to be proud of such a religion." —"ABOUT THE GRIEFS OF THE MANGS AND MAHARS"

FEBRUARY 17, 1958 The Campaign for Nuclear Disarmament is founded in Britain; it would become the country's most important protest movement during the late 1950s and early 1960s.

FEBRUARY 18, 1934 Black lesbian poet Audre Lorde is born in New York City.

"For all of us
this instant and this triumph
We were never meant to survive."
—"A LITANY FOR SURVIVAL"

FEBRUARY 19, 1942 Japanese American internment begins in the US through Executive Order 9066.

FEBRUARY 19, 1963 Betty Friedan's _The Feminine Mystique_, a classic of second-wave feminism, is published. "The problem lay buried, unspoken, for many years in the minds of American women."

WEDNESDAY FEBRUARY 17

Audre Lorde © Robert Alexander, 1983

THURSDAY FEBRUARY 18

NOTES:

FRIDAY FEBRUARY 19

SATURDAY FEBRUARY 20

V

TO SPEAK OF CRISIS MEANS THEN TO ASK THE QUESTION, A CRISIS FOR WHOM?
EMMA DOWLING

The restructuring of welfare states in Europe and North American is but one facet of a manifest global care crisis within and across societies in which a growing number of the world's population cannot access the care and subsistence they require. This is a crisis that affects access to care as well as the work that goes into its provision. To get a sense of the dimensions of the global need for care, in 2015 there were an estimated 2.1 billion people worldwide in need of care, predominantly children (the overwhelming majority) and the elderly. By 2030, the total is expected to rise to 2.3 billion. However, care for these recipients is increasingly difficult to ensure.

While the number of the world's population unable to satisfy basic care needs grows, so too does care inequality not just within, but across, societies. Where Global North countries display dramatic differences in access to care, developing countries face a situation where a lack of health care infrastructure exacerbates the challenges of chronic illness, epidemics, natural disasters and conflict. Part of the crisis of care is also the plight of refugees and those countries along the borders of the European Union, already struggling with insufficient social infrastructures and having to respond to the needs of migrants fleeing war, persecution and economic deprivation. According to the United Nations Refugee Agency, in 2016 there were an unprecedented 65.6 million people forced from their homes worldwide, over half of whom were under the age of eighteen. When refugees—adults and children—drown in the Mediterranean, some people in prospective host countries even dare to suggest that they should not be cared for, in case that would motivate more people to come.

So often, the problems we face as a society are couched in economic terms, with all else appearing as derivative: get "the economy" back on track, facilitate economic growth—that is how to address the pressing issues of our time, be this climate change and environmental degradation or social inequality, exclusion or need. However, were we to change our view and look at the economy from the perspective of care, our debates would change with regard to the problems we face and the solutions to them on a local and global scale.

When we think of care we usually think of individual sentiments or behaviours—the feeling of caring *about* someone or the act of caring *for* someone; or even the state of the world. Yet, individual intentions and individual actions appear insufficient in the face of the overwhelming problems of our time. It feels a bit futile—naïve even—to believe in the possibilities of everyone just being that little bit nicer to each other in an attempt to bring about a better world. It is so painfully obvious that massive economic disparities and major political power imbalances are what characterize our present predicament. Can something so seemingly fragile as care be powerful enough to transform these? Acts of kindness may make us feel better, but can they really be both the means and end for change? And it is not just the cynics who are suspicious of the imposition of an imperative to care. Ways of caring can also be patronizing and confining. Immediately, the questions arise: who defines? Who decides? Who enforces? And how?

In an unequal world, no crisis affects everyone in the same way. To speak of crisis means then to ask the question, *a crisis for whom*? It means to speak of class and inequality in the way that the crisis is experienced, and in the way that care is organized to entrench division and pit us against one another. It means asking: who is cared for and who is not?

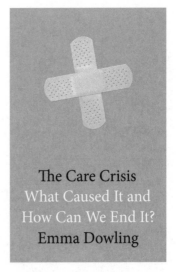

The Care Crisis
What Caused It and
How Can We End It?
Emma Dowling

This is a revised extract from The Care Crisis: Who Caused It And How Can We End It *by Emma Dowling (Verso, 2020).*

SUNDAY FEBRUARY 21

MONDAY FEBRUARY 22

TUESDAY FEBRUARY 23

FEBRUARY 21, 1848 The *Communist Manifesto*, written by Friedrich Engels and Karl Marx, is published. "The proletarians have nothing to lose but their chains. They have a world to win."

FEBRUARY 21, 1965 Malcolm X is assassinated at the Audubon Ballroom in New York City. "Uncle Sam's hands are dripping with blood, dripping with the blood of the black man in this country." —"THE BALLOT OR THE BULLET"

FEBRUARY 23, 1934 George Padmore, leading Pan-Africanist born in Trinidad, is expelled from the Comintern and shifts his focus to African independence struggles. "The black man certainly has to pay dear for carrying the white man's burden." —"THE WHITE MAN'S BURDEN"

FEBRUARY 26, 1906 Upton Sinclair's exposé on the meat packing industry, *The Jungle*, is published, prompting the enactment of the Meat Inspection and Pure Food and Drug Acts.

FEBRUARY 27, 1832 Auguste Blanqui, French revolutionary and early theorist of class struggle, is found guilty (with fourteen others) of supporting republicanism. "This is the war between the rich and the poor: the rich wanted it so, for they are the aggressors. But they find it wrong that the poor fight back." —BLANQUI'S DEFENSE SPEECH

FEBRUARY 27, 1973 Oglala Lakota and American Indian Movement members, including Leonard Peltier, begin an occupation of Wounded Knee, South Dakota on the Pine Ridge Indian Reservation.

WEDNESDAY FEBRUARY 24

Malcolm X (1925–1965) by Ed Ford, World Telegram staff photographer

THURSDAY FEBRUARY 25

NOTES:

FRIDAY FEBRUARY 26

SATURDAY FEBRUARY 27

SUNDAY FEBRUARY 28

MONDAY MARCH 01

TUESDAY MARCH 02

MARCH 1, 1896 Ethiopian fighters defeat Italian forces at the Battle of Adwa, securing Ethiopian sovereignty to become a symbol of African resistance against European colonialism. "Once a white snake has bitten you, you will find no cure for it." —ETHIOPIAN REBEL LEADER BAHTA HAGOS

MARCH 1, 1940 Richard Wright's seminal novel *Native Son*, about a black youth living on Chicago's South Side, is published. His writings would shift the US discourse on race.

"FB eye under my bed
Told me all I dreamed last night, every word I said."
—"FB EYE BLUES"

MARCH 1, 1954 Lolita Lebrón and comrades open fire on the US House of Representatives in the struggle for Puerto Rican independence. "I did not come to kill anyone, I came to die for Puerto Rico." —LEBRÓN, WORDS UPON ARREST

MARCH 2, 1444 Albanian resistance leader Skanderbeg founds the League of Lezhë, uniting Balkan chieftains to fight the invading Ottoman army.

MARCH 6, 1923 The Egyptian Feminist Union is established. "They rise in times of trouble when the wills of men are tried." —ACTIVIST HUDA SHAARAWI, *HAREM YEARS: THE MEMOIRS OF AN EGYPTIAN FEMINIST, 1879–1924*

MARCH 6, 1957 The leader of the Gold Coast's imperialism fight against the British, Pan-Africanist Kwame Nkrumah, becomes the first prime minister of independent Ghana.

MARCH 6, 1984 Coal miners walk out at Cortonwood Colliery in South Yorkshire, beginning the yearlong UK miner's strike, the longest in history. "I'd rather be a picket than a scab." —PICKET LINE SLOGAN

WEDNESDAY MARCH 03

Lolita Lebrón (1919–2010) following her arrest in 1954

THURSDAY MARCH 04

NOTES:

FRIDAY MARCH 05

SATURDAY MARCH 06

SUNDAY MARCH 07

_____

_____

_____

_____

_____

_____

_____

MONDAY MARCH 08

_____

_____

_____

_____

_____

_____

_____

TUESDAY MARCH 09

_____

_____

_____

_____

_____

_____

_____

MARCH 7, 1921 At the Kronstadt naval base, Russia's Red Army attacks sailors, soldiers and civilians who are protesting widespread famine and the Bolshevik repression of strikes. "This unrest shows clearly enough that the party has lost the faith of the working masses." —PETROPAVLOVSK RESOLUTION AND DEMANDS

MARCH 7, 1942 Lucy Parsons, anarchist and Industrial Workers of the World cofounder who was born in slavery, dies in Chicago. "Stroll you down the avenues of the rich and look through the magnificent plate windows into their voluptuous homes, and here you will discover the _very identical robbers_ who have despoiled you and yours." —"TO TRAMPS"

MARCH 8, 1914 First International Women's Day, cofounded by German Marxist Clara Zetkin, is established on this day of the year. "What made women's labour particularly attractive to the capitalists was not only its lower price but also the greater submissiveness of women."

MARCH 12, 1930 Mohandas Gandhi begins the Salt Satyagraha, challenging the British Raj. "I know the dangers attendant upon the methods adopted by me. But the country is not likely to mistake my meaning."

MARCH 13, 1933 The poet Abdukhaliq Uyghur is executed by the Chinese government for encouraging rebellion and supporting Uyghur independence.

MARCH 13, 1979 Maurice Bishop's New Jewel Movement overthrows the Grenada government, the first armed socialist revolution in a predominantly black country outside of Africa. "The true meaning of revolutionary democracy ... is a growth in fraternal love."

WEDNESDAY MARCH 10

_____
_____
_____
_____
_____
_____
_____

Lucy Parsons (1853–1942) after her arrest for rioting at a 1915 unemployment protest

THURSDAY MARCH 11

_____
_____
_____
_____
_____
_____
_____

NOTES:

_____
_____
_____
_____
_____
_____

FRIDAY MARCH 12

_____
_____
_____
_____
_____
_____
_____

SATURDAY MARCH 13

_____
_____
_____
_____
_____
_____
_____

SUNDAY MARCH 14

MONDAY MARCH 15

TUESDAY MARCH 16

MARCH 14, 2008 Riots break out in Lhasa and spread throughout Tibet, targeting Han Chinese residents and businesses. "The oppressors' snipers are still standing above Tibetan people's heads; on sunny days, the beams deflected from the guns in their hands stab into the prostrating Tibetans. This is a collective memory which has been engraved on Tibetan people's hearts."
—TIBETAN POET WOESER

MARCH 15, 1845 Friedrich Engels publishes *The Condition of the Working Class in England*.

MARCH 15, 1960 A student demonstration against the fraudulent election victory of South Korean strongman Syngman Rhee was attacked by police. One month later, the body of student protester Kim Ju-yul washed ashore, his skull split open by a tear-gas grenade. The public outrage would eventually result in the April Revolution, which would end Rhee's rule.

MARCH 18, 1834 Six farm workers from Tolpuddle, England, are sentenced to penal transportation to Australia for forming a trade union. "Labour is the poor man's property, from which all protection is withheld. Has not then the working man as much right to preserve and protect his labour as the rich man has his capital?" —TOLPUDDLE MARTYR GEORGE LOVELESS, *THE VICTIMS OF WHIGGERY*

MARCH 18, 1871 Paris Commune is established, a participatory workers' democracy. "Workers, make no mistake—this is an all-out war, a war between parasites and workers, exploiters and producers."
—COMMUNARDS, "DECLARATION BY THE CENTRAL COMMITTEE OF THE NATIONAL GUARD"

MARCH 19, 2005 First road blockade in Kennedy Road settlement in Durban, South Africa, that would become the Abahlali baseMjondolo ("shack dwellers") movement.

WEDNESDAY MARCH 17

Paris Commune: a barricade on Rue Voltaire, after its capture by the regular army during the Bloody Week

THURSDAY MARCH 18

NOTES:

FRIDAY MARCH 19

SATURDAY MARCH 20

SUNDAY MARCH 21

MONDAY MARCH 22

TUESDAY MARCH 23

MARCH 21, 1960 South African police kill sixty-nine protesters in the Sharpeville Massacre, forcing the anti-apartheid movement underground.

MARCH 23, 1918 Avant-garde artist Tristan Tzara issues the Dada Manifesto, a politico-artistic movement whose anti-bourgeois stance would influence the Situationists and the Beats. "DADA DADA DADA—the roar of contorted pains, the interweaving of contraries and all contradictions, freaks and irrelevancies: LIFE."

MARCH 23, 1931 Revolutionary Bhagat Singh, who threw a bomb into India's central legislative assembly, is hanged by the British Raj. "Let me tell you, British rule is here not because God wills it but because they possess power and we do not dare to oppose them." —"WHY AM I AN ATHEIST?"

MARCH 24, 1987 First demonstration of ACT UP, pioneering direct-action AIDS organization, on Wall Street to protest Food and Drug Administration inaction on drug development. "Silence = Death" —ACT UP LOGO

MARCH 27, 1969 First national Chicano Youth Conference is hosted in Denver by Crusade for Justice, the civil rights organization founded by former boxer Corky Gonzáles.

"I have come a long way to nowhere,
  unwillingly dragged by that
  monstrous, technical,
  industrial giant
  called
  Progress
  and Anglo success ..."
   —GONZÁLES, "I AM JOAQUIN"

WEDNESDAY MARCH 24

_____
_____
_____
_____
_____
_____
_____

SILENCE=DEATH

The iconic poster of ACT UP, 1987

THURSDAY MARCH 25

_____
_____
_____
_____
_____
_____
_____

NOTES:

_____
_____
_____
_____
_____
_____

FRIDAY MARCH 26

_____
_____
_____
_____
_____
_____
_____

SATURDAY MARCH 27

_____
_____
_____
_____
_____
_____

Dignity for the Earth by Meredith Stern (Justseeds Artists Coop/justseeds.org)

Time to Connect by Josh MacPhee (Justseeds Artists Coop/justseeds.org)

SUNDAY MARCH 28

MONDAY MARCH 29

TUESDAY MARCH 30

MARCH 29, 1942 The Hukbalahap (Philippine communist guerrilla organization) is founded; its insurgency against the government lasts eight years. "Our friends in Manila refer to us as being 'outside.' That is incorrect terminology ... We are on the inside of the struggle." —PEASANT LEADER LUIS TARUC, *BORN OF THE PEOPLE*

MARCH 30, 1892 Freethinker Robert Ingersoll, favorite orator of Walt Whitman, delivers a eulogy for the poet after his death. "Whoever produces anything by weary labor, does not need a revelation from heaven to teach him that he has a right to the thing produced." —INGERSOLL, "SOME MISTAKES OF MOSES"

APRIL 1, 1649 Poor farmers begin digging plots at Saint George's Hill in Surrey, in one of the first acts of the Digger movement that sought to abolish property and wages, in some instances by occupying common land. "We are resolved to be cheated no longer, nor be held under the slavish fear of you no longer, seeing the Earth was made for us, as well as for you." —MOVEMENT FOUNDER GERRARD WINSTANLEY, "DECLARATION FROM THE POOR OPPRESSED PEOPLE OF ENGLAND"

APRIL 3, 1874 Wong Chin Foo, publisher of the first Chinese American newspaper, is naturalized as a US citizen. "The difference between the heathen and the Christian is that the heathen does good for the sake of doing good."

APRIL 3, 1895 Playwright and essayist Oscar Wilde goes on trial for homosexual activity and is imprisoned for two years. "It is immoral to use private property in order to alleviate the horrible evils that result from the institution of private property." —"THE SOUL OF MAN UNDER SOCIALISM"

THE SOUL OF MAN UNDER SOCIALISM.

THE chief advantage that would result from the establishment of
Socialism is, undoubtedly, the fact that Socialism would relieve us
from that sordid necessity of living for others which, in the present
condition of things, presses so hardly upon almost everybody. In
fact, scarcely anyone at all escapes.

Now and then, in the course of the century, a great man of
science, like Darwin; a great poet, like Keats; a fine critical spirit,
like M. Renan; a supreme artist, like Flaubert, has been able to
isolate himself, to keep himself out of reach of the clamorous claims
of others, to stand "under the shelter of the wall," as Plato puts it,
and so to realise the perfection of what was in him, to his own
incomparable gain, and to the incomparable and lasting gain of the
whole world. These, however, are exceptions. The majority of
people spoil their lives by an unhealthy and exaggerated altruism—
are forced, indeed, so to spoil them. They find themselves surrounded
by hideous poverty, by hideous ugliness, by hideous starvation. It
is inevitable that they should be strongly moved by all this. The
emotions of man are stirred more quickly than man's intelligence;
and, as I pointed out some time ago in an article on the function of
criticism, it is much more easy to have sympathy with suffering than

"The Soul of Man under Socialism" by Oscar Wilde. First publication in *Fortnightly Review*, February 1891

THURSDAY APRIL 01

NOTES:

FRIDAY APRIL 02

SATURDAY APRIL 03

APRIL 4, 1968 Martin Luther King, Jr. is assassinated. "A true revolution of values will soon look uneasily on the glaring contrast of poverty and wealth." —"BEYOND VIETNAM: A TIME TO BREAK SILENCE"

APRIL 5, 1971 The "Manifesto of the 343," signed by 343 women (including Simone de Beauvoir) who had had secret abortions, demands that the French government legalize the procedure.

APRIL 5, 1976 On the traditional day of mourning, thousands of Beijingers lay wreaths and poems on Tiananmen Square, indirectly criticizing the Cultural Revolution.

"If a thousand challengers lie beneath your feet, Count me as number thousand and one."
—BEI DAO, "THE ANSWER," WHICH BECAME AN ANTHEM OF THE DEMOCRACY MOVEMENT

APRIL 8, 1950 Imprisoned for sedition, the revolutionary Turkish poet Nazim Hikmet launches a hunger strike for amnesty for political prisoners.

"Galloping from farthest Asia
and jutting into the Mediterranean
like a mare's head
this country is ours."
—"INVITATION"

APRIL 9, 1553 François Rabelais dies; he is the author of *Gargantua and Pantagruel*, an early modern novel that subverted the Renaissance social order.

APRIL 10, 1919 Emiliano Zapata, Mexican Revolution leader, is assassinated by the government. "The nation is tired of false men and traitors who make promises like liberators and who on arriving in power forget them and constitute themselves as tyrants."

WEDNESDAY APRIL 07

Dr. Martin Luther King, Jr. (1929–1968) being arrested in 1956
during the Montgomery Bus Boycott

THURSDAY APRIL 08

NOTES:

FRIDAY APRIL 09

SATURDAY APRIL 10

SUNDAY APRIL 11

MONDAY APRIL 12

TUESDAY APRIL 13

APRIL 11, 1981 Riots break out in the Caribbean London neighborhood of Brixton in response to police targeting of young black men under the Sus law. The fighting lasts for three days.

APRIL 11, 2007 Kurt Vonnegut, author of novels with anti-authoritarian and anti-war themes, dies.

APRIL 13, 1635 Fakhr al-Din II, Druze independence leader against the Ottoman Empire and Lebanon's first freedom fighter, is executed. "No promise of reward or threat of punishment will dissuade us." —MESSAGE TO THE PEOPLE

APRIL 14, 1428 Vietnamese forces are victorious after a ten-year rebellion against their Chinese rulers. "Today it is a case of the grasshopper pitted against the elephant. But tomorrow the elephant will have its guts ripped out." —REBELLION LEADER LÊ LỢI'S VICTORY SPEECH

APRIL 14, 2002 Venezuelan president Hugo Chávez, who described his socialist movement as the Bolivarian Revolution, returns to power after having been ousted in a US-backed coup two days earlier. "What we now have to do is define the future of the world. Dawn is breaking out all over." —ADDRESS TO THE UN GENERAL ASSEMBLY

APRIL 15, 1936 The Great Revolt begins in Palestine against British Mandate and Zionism, lasting three years. "They stepped all over us until we couldn't take any more. This went on until the rebellion was smashed." —MAHMOUD ABOU DEEB, WITNESS TO THE REVOLT

WEDNESDAY APRIL 14

The Brixton Riots, 1981

THURSDAY APRIL 15

NOTES:

FRIDAY APRIL 16

SATURDAY APRIL 17

SUNDAY APRIL 18

_____

_____

_____

_____

_____

_____

_____

MONDAY APRIL 19

_____

_____

_____

_____

_____

_____

TUESDAY APRIL 20

_____

_____

_____

_____

_____

_____

APRIL 20, 1773 Peter Bestes and others deliver a petition for freedom "in behalf of our fellow slaves" to the Massachusetts legislature. "The divine spirit of freedom seems to fire every human breast on the continent, except such as are bribed to assist in executing the execrable plan."

APRIL 21, 1913 The Indian revolutionary group, the Ghadar Party, is formed by Punjabis in North America. "The nation-state may truly be compared to the dinosaurs and the tyrannosaurus of the Mesozoic Age. Like those gigantic reptiles, the modern nation-state has a very small brain with which to think and plan, but tremendously powerful teeth with which to tear and rend, to destroy and dismember." —FOUNDER LALA HAR DAYAL, "HINTS OF SELF-CULTURE"

APRIL 22, 1977 Kenyan activist Wangari Maathai founds the Green Belt Movement, an environmental nonprofit aimed at empowering poor, rural women. "Until you dig a hole, you plant a tree, you water it and make it survive, you haven't done a thing."

APRIL 23, 1968 Students occupy buildings in New York's Columbia University to protest the school's ties to a defense contractor, triggering a campus-wide strike. "Up against the wall, Motherfuckers!" —PROTEST GRAFFITI

APRIL 24, 1916 Irish republicans mount an armed insurrection against the British imperialists on Easter week, in what became known as the Easter Rising.

WEDNESDAY APRIL 21

POBLACHT NA H EIREANN.
THE PROVISIONAL GOVERNMENT
OF THE
IRISH REPUBLIC
TO THE PEOPLE OF IRELAND.

IRISHMEN AND IRISHWOMEN: In the name of God and of the dead generations from which she receives her old tradition of nationhood, Ireland, through us, summons her children to her flag and strikes for her freedom.

Having organised and trained her manhood through her secret revolutionary organisation, the Irish Republican Brotherhood, and through her open military organisations, the Irish Volunteers and the Irish Citizen Army; having patiently perfected her discipline, having resolutely waited for the right moment to reveal itself, she now seizes that moment, and, supported by her exiled children in America and by gallant allies in Europe, but relying in the first on her own strength, she strikes in full confidence of victory.

We declare the right of the people of Ireland to the ownership of Ireland, and to the unfettered control of Irish destinies, to be sovereign and indefeasible. The long usurpation of that right by a foreign people and government has not extinguished the right, nor can it ever be extinguished except by the destruction of the Irish people. In every generation the Irish people have asserted their right to national freedom and sovereignty: six times during the past three hundred years they have asserted it in arms. Standing on that fundamental right, and again asserting it in arms in the face of the world, we hereby proclaim the Irish Republic as a Sovereign Independent State, and we pledge our lives and the lives of our comrades-in-arms to the cause of its freedom, of its welfare, and of its exaltation among the nations.

The Proclamation of the Irish Republic, 1916

THURSDAY APRIL 22

NOTES:

FRIDAY APRIL 23

SATURDAY APRIL 24

FEMINIST AND ANTI-CARCERAL MOVEMENTS
MUST CONFRONT THE SEX OFFENSE LEGAL REGIME
JUDITH LEVINE AND ERICA R. MEINERS

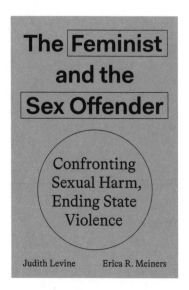

The Feminist and the Sex Offender

Confronting Sexual Harm, Ending State Violence

Judith Levine   Erica R. Meiners

"The people on the front lines against violence against women should also be on the front lines of abolitionist struggles," declared Angela Davis in a 2014 speech. And those "opposed to police crimes should be opposed to domestic—privatized—violence."

Feminist and anti-carceral movements must squarely confront the sex offense legal regime because it embodies some of the criminal legal system's cruelest practices. But there are other, less obvious reasons as well. For instance, the registry is designed to produce shame, and shame feeds a culture of sexual and gender violence and inhibits its survivors from speaking up.

Unfortunately, only rarely do people working in abolitionist and feminist struggles connect with those working against the sex offense legal regime. Focused in their daily practice on their "own" issues, these folks do not always cooperate, much less collaborate, with one another. People in the broad prison-industrial-complex abolitionist movement often marginalize or even openly denigrate those convicted of sex crimes. So do majority-white progressive movements; Occupy Boston, for instance, was riven by proposals to ban people on the registry from the encampment. None of this is particularly surprising. After all, social justice activists' anxieties about sex are no less acute than anyone else's.

For their part, the small network of "sex offenders" and their families working for the rights of "registered citizens" and those of the incarcerated or civilly committed for sex offenses do not generally have a robust critique of the prison nation. We often hear a mother say: "There are some people who should be in prison / civil commitment / on the registry—the worst of the worst. But my son is not one of them." On their websites, registrants' rights activists always stress the importance of preventing sexual harm, but too often they minimize the pain of those, particularly women and girls, who have been harmed. These two movements also stand, for the most part, on two sides of a racial divide. Activists against the prison industrial complex are more likely to be nonwhite, while those advocating for men on the registry are mostly white. Moreover, neither has broadly embraced feminism. For many on the registry, feminism is public enemy number one. More than a few in the movement to abolish the prison-industrial complex—men, but also women—simply disregard feminism, considering it irrelevant to their struggle.

And no major resistance movement foregrounds pleasure and everyday happiness as primary progressive concerns. Even to accomplish their own identified goals, these movements—feminism, registrants' rights, and prison abolition—need to understand each other's issues as akin to their own and find ways to come together in common struggles. Toward that end, one of our aims is to scrutinize some of the major conflicts between and among these movements and propose potential alliances. We neither contend that these conflicts are unjustified nor pretend that they can all be resolved. But opening lines of communication can help these now separate movements find a shared analysis and build the solidarity without which none of us will win.

We can make a world that is safer, freer, and happier: one in which domination and violence are universally condemned and all can flourish. That may sound like a utopian, even deluded, statement. But, as every organizer knows, you can't plot a route unless you know where you want to arrive. Organizing for social justice is not a matter of settling for one or the other—of dreaming of heaven or living on earth. What we have learned from the people whose brilliance is reflected in these pages is that a better world is not a destination, but a road. It is not a place, but a practice.

This is a revised extract from The Feminist and the Sex Offender: Confronting Sexual Harm, Ending State Violence *by Judith Levine and Erica R. Meiners (Verso, 2020).*

SUNDAY APRIL 25

_____

_____

_____

_____

_____

_____

_____

MONDAY APRIL 26

_____

_____

_____

_____

_____

_____

_____

TUESDAY APRIL 27

_____

_____

_____

_____

_____

_____

_____

APRIL 25, 1974 Portuguese armed forces overthrow the ruling Estado Novo dictatorship in what becomes known as the Carnation Revolution, setting the stage for its colonies to achieve independence.

APRIL 26, 1937 The Basque town of Guernica is destroyed in an aerial bombing by German and Italian forces, in one of the most sordid episodes of the Spanish Civil War.

"Faces good in firelight good in frost
Refusing the night the wounds and blows."
—SURREALIST POET PAUL ELUARD, "VICTORY OF GUERNICA"

APRIL 28, 1967 Heavyweight champion boxer Muhammad Ali refuses induction into the US Armed Forces, leading to a charge for draft evasion and being stripped of his titles. "I ain't got no quarrel with them Vietcong. No Vietcong ever called me nigger."

APRIL 29, 1992 Los Angeles residents begin rioting after the four police officers accused of beating Rodney King are acquitted. "Give us the hammer and the nails, we will rebuild the city." —BLOODS AND CRIPS, "PLAN FOR THE RECONSTRUCTION OF LOS ANGELES"

MAY 1, 1949 Albert Einstein publishes "Why Socialism?" in the inaugural issue of _Monthly Review._ "The economic anarchy of capitalist society as it exists today is, in my opinion, the real source of the evil."

MAY 1, 1970 Lesbian activists deliver their manifesto at the Second Congress to Unite Women in New York City, to protest the exclusion of lesbian speakers. "Lesbian is a label invented by the man to throw at any woman who dares to be his equal." —RADICALESBIANS, "THE WOMAN-IDENTIFIED WOMAN"

WEDNESDAY APRIL 28

_____

_____

_____

_____

_____

_____

_____

Boxer and conscientious objector Muhammad Ali in 1966

THURSDAY APRIL 29

_____

_____

_____

_____

_____

_____

_____

NOTES:

_____

_____

_____

_____

_____

_____

FRIDAY APRIL 30

_____

_____

_____

_____

_____

_____

_____

SATURDAY MAY 01

_____

_____

_____

_____

_____

_____

_____

SUNDAY MAY 02

_____

_____

_____

_____

_____

_____

MONDAY MAY 03

_____

_____

_____

_____

_____

_____

TUESDAY MAY 04

_____

_____

_____

_____

_____

_____

MAY 3, 1968 French students protest the closure of the Sorbonne, setting off the May '68 wave of demonstrations and strikes by millions of students and workers. "Be realistic, demand the impossible." —PARIS GRAFFITI

MAY 4, 1886 At a rally for the eight-hour day at Haymarket Square in Chicago, a bomb is thrown at police and eight anarchists are later convicted of conspiracy. "I repeat that I am the enemy of the 'order' of today, and I repeat that, with all my powers, so long as breath remains in me, I shall combat it." —LOUIS LINGG'S TRIAL SPEECH

MAY 4, 1919 Chinese students demonstrate in Beijing, sparking the anti-Confucian New Culture Movement. "Wanting to eat men, at the same time afraid of being eaten themselves, they all eye each other with the deepest suspicion." —LU XUN, _A MADMAN'S DIARY_, ONE OF THE MOVEMENT'S REPRESENTATIVE WORKS

MAY 5, 1938 Second and final arrest of Russian poet Osip Mandelstam, for writing critically of Stalin.

"He forges decrees in a line like horseshoes
One for the groin, one the forehead, temple, eye"
—"THE STALIN EPIGRAM"

MAY 5, 1966 Jit Poumisak, Thai Marxist poet and revolutionary, is killed after retreating to the jungle with the outlawed Communist Party. "[The Thai people] have been able to identify clearly the enemies who plunder them and skin them alive and suck the very marrow from their bones." —"THE REAL FACE OF THAI SAKTINA [FEUDALISM] TODAY"

WEDNESDAY MAY 05

The first flier calling for a rally in the Haymarket on May 4, 1886

THURSDAY MAY 06

NOTES:

FRIDAY MAY 07

SATURDAY MAY 08

SUNDAY MAY 09

_____

_____

_____

_____

_____

MONDAY MAY 10

_____

_____

_____

_____

_____

TUESDAY MAY 11

_____

_____

_____

_____

_____

_____

MAY 9, 1918 Scottish revolutionary John Maclean, on trial for sedition for opposing WWI, delivers a rousing speech from the dock. "I am here as the accuser of capitalism, dripping with blood from head to foot."

MAY 11, 1930 Pedro Albizu Campos is elected president of the Puerto Rican Nationalist Party. "The empire is a system. It can wait. It can fatten its victims to render its digestion more enjoyable at a later time."

MAY 10, 1857 Rebellion against British rule in India begins, eventually growing into the First Indian War of Independence.

MAY 10, 1872 Victoria Woodhull, suffragist and publisher of the first English edition of _The Communist Manifesto_, becomes the first woman nominated for president of the US.

MAY 11, 1894 Three thousand employees of the Pullman railcar company go on strike, eventually growing to 250,000 workers before being crushed by federal troops.

MAY 12, 1916 James Connolly is tied to a chair and shot by the British government for his role in the Easter Rising—the precursor to the declaration of the Irish Republic in 1919. Born in Scotland to Irish immigrant parents, Connolly became a leader of the socialist movement in Scotland, Ireland and the United States, where he was a member of the Socialist Party and the IWW.

MAY 13, 1968 French workers join students in a one-day strike, with over a million protesters marching through Paris streets. By the following week, two-thirds of France's workforce was on strike, becoming the largest general strike that had ever stopped the economy of an industrialized country.

WEDNESDAY MAY 12

_____

_____

_____

_____

_____

_____

_____

Victoria Woodhull, suffragist and publisher of the first English edition of _The Communist Manifesto_

THURSDAY MAY 13

NOTES:

FRIDAY MAY 14

SATURDAY MAY 15

SUNDAY MAY 16

_____

_____

_____

_____

_____

_____

_____

_____

MONDAY MAY 17

_____

_____

_____

_____

_____

_____

_____

TUESDAY MAY 18

_____

_____

_____

_____

_____

_____

MAY 16, 1943 Warsaw Ghetto Uprising, which began in German-occupied Poland to resist the last deportation of Jews to the Treblinka extermination camp, ends in failure. "We decided to gamble for our lives." —MAREK EDELMAN, MEMBER OF THE JEWISH COMBAT ORGANIZATION

MAY 17, 1649 A mutiny in the New Model Army of England by the Levellers, who called for the expansion of suffrage, religious toleration, and sweeping political reforms, is crushed when its leaders are executed. "We do now hold ourselves bound in mutual duty to each other to take the best care we can for the future to avoid both the danger of returning into a slavish condition and the chargeable remedy of another war." —LEVELLERS, "AGREEMENT OF THE PEOPLE"

MAY 18, 1980 Citizens of Kwangju, South Korea, seize control of their city, demanding democratization, an end to martial law, and an increase in the minimum wage.

MAY 19, 1863 US president Ulysses S. Grant issues the National Eight Hour Law Proclamation, an early but symbolic victory for the struggle over the working day in the US. "Think carefully of the difference between the operative and the mechanic leaving his work at half-past seven (after dark, the most of the year), and that of the more leisurely walk home at half-past four p.m., or three hours earlier." —MACHINIST-TURNED-ACTIVIST IRA STEWARD, "THE EIGHT HOUR MOVEMENT"

MAY 19, 1946 Millions of Japanese take part in the Food May Day demonstrations, protesting the country's broken food delivery system.

WEDNESDAY MAY 19

Children participating in the protest known as Food May Day for food supplies in Japan, 1946

THURSDAY MAY 20

NOTES:

FRIDAY MAY 21

SATURDAY MAY 22

SUNDAY MAY 23

MONDAY MAY 24

TUESDAY MAY 25

MAY 25, 1899 Bengal's "rebel poet" Kazi Nazrul Islam is born.

> "And I shall rest, battle-weary rebel, only on the day
> when the wails of the oppressed shall not rend the air and sky."
>
> —"THE REBEL"

MAY 28, 1913 Six hundred black women march through Bloemfontein, South Africa to protest the law requiring them, as non-white workers, to carry proof of employment.

> "Too long have they submitted
> to white malignity;
> No passes they would carry
> but assert their dignity."
>
> —POEM INSPIRED BY THE EVENT, SIGNED "JOHNNY THE OFFICE BOY"

MAY 28, 1918 First Republic of Armenia is declared, following the Armenian Resistance of 1914–18.

MAY 29, 1851 Sojourner Truth, abolitionist speaker, delivers her famous "Ain't I a Woman" speech to the Women's Convention in Akron, Ohio. "I can't read, but I can hear. I have heard the Bible and I learned that Eve caused man to sin. Well, if woman upset the world, do give her a chance to set it right again."

MAY 29, 1963 Peruvian revolutionary Hugo Blanco is captured after leading a "Land or Death" peasant uprising that sparked the country's first agrarian reform. Blanco was spared from execution thanks to pleas from Bertrand Russell, Jean-Paul Sartre, Simone de Beauvoir, Che Guevara, and others. "To be a revolutionary is to love the world, to love life, to be happy."
—"TO MY PEOPLE," WRITTEN FROM EL FRONTÓN PENAL COLONY

WEDNESDAY MAY 26

_____

_____

_____

_____

_____

_____

_____

Armenian Revolutionary Federation fighters, banner reading
"Liberty or Death"

THURSDAY MAY 27

_____

_____

_____

_____

_____

_____

_____

NOTES:

_____

_____

_____

_____

_____

_____

FRIDAY MAY 28

_____

_____

_____

_____

_____

_____

_____

SATURDAY MAY 29

_____

_____

_____

_____

_____

_____

_____

V

GIMME SHELTER
JOHN WASHINGTON

The basic idea of asylum is simple. Someone comes to your door because they are in danger, because they are afraid. You open your door, and you share your roof. But within this simple idea lies a labyrinth constructed of different sorts of fear: some fear is grounded in immediate physical danger, some is diffused in general conditions of oppression; some is exaggerated, some completely imagined. Some fears are unrealized, some send you to your grave.

As a legal construct, asylum is less simple. According to the 1951 UN Refugee Convention, which set the original international standard for defining refugees and asylum seekers, an asylum seeker is someone who, "owing to a well-founded fear of being persecuted for reasons of race, religion, nationality, membership of a particular social group or political opinion, is outside the country of his nationality and is unable or, owing to such fear, is unwilling to avail himself of the protection of that country;

or who, not having a nationality and being outside the country of his former habitual residence as a result of such events, is unable or, owing to such fear, is unwilling to return to it."

Fear is the requisite for asylum, but the definition is based on a fear of a specific entity, the state—a fear of being persecuted by the state or its representatives. But the fear must be "well founded," and many of today's asylum seekers, especially those from Central America and Mexico (where, taken together, most people seeking asylum in the United States are from), are fleeing non-state persecutors. The single country from which most asylum seekers come to the United States in recent years has been China, though in 2018 Venezuela topped the list for the first time.

According to the United Nations High Commissioner for Refugees' (UNHCR) Handbook on Procedures and Criteria for Determining Refugee Status, "in general, the applicant's

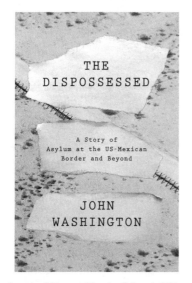

THE
DISPOSSESSED

A Story of
Asylum at the US-Mexican
Border and Beyond

JOHN
WASHINGTON

fear should be considered well founded if he can establish, to a reasonable degree, that his continued stay in his country of origin has become intolerable to him."

The US Supreme Court also wrestled with the definition of well-founded fear after adopting the language of the Refugee Convention into law with the 1980 Refugee Act. During the oral argument for a 1987 case, *Immigration and Naturalization Service v. Cardoza-Fonseca*, in which a Nicaraguan woman who overstayed her visa appealed to the United States for asylum, attorney Dana Leigh Marks (now an immigration judge) suggested defining such fear according to the "reasonable person" standard: would a "reasonable person" in this same factual situation fear persecution upon return to their country? But the justices sought a more quantifiable criterion than reasonableness—they tried to pin down the quivering subjectivity of fear. In his majority opinion Justice John Paul Stevens wrote, "One can certainly have a well-founded fear of an event happening when there is less than a 50 percent chance of the occurrence taking place."

Politically, the modern concept of asylum—though rooted in ancient religious traditions of sanctuary and primordial codes of welcoming the stranger—was formed in a period of political statecrafting and Cold War geopolitical braggadocio. Today's legal concepts of refugee and asylum laws are still based on definitions that were originally tightly circumscribed by anti-communist ideology.

Amid the postbellum shuffle and rethink, the asylum policies enshrined in the 1951 Refugee Convention only applied to Europeans who were forced to flee their homes by events occurring before January 1, 1951, though hundreds of thousands had been similarly uprooted and unroofed in Asia and Africa, and millions more would take wing in subsequent years. These geographical and temporal limitations were more about politics than about need or even capacity. As Matthew Gibney puts it, "No country knit together its definition of a refugee with escape from communism as tightly as the US. Before 1980, refugees from non-communist countries (with the sole exception of the Middle East) had no status under US law." Accepting refugees and asylum seekers was a way for the United States to leak the communist bloc of its citizens and undermine their governments. Those fleeing the rest of the world were simply left in the cold.

This is a revised extract from The Dispossessed: A Story of Asylum and the US-Mexican Border and Beyond *by John Washington (Verso, 2020).*

SUNDAY MAY 30

_____

_____

_____

_____

_____

_____

_____

_____

MONDAY MAY 31

_____

_____

_____

_____

_____

_____

_____

TUESDAY JUNE 01

_____

_____

_____

_____

_____

_____

_____

JUNE 4, 1450 Jack Cade, who led 5,000 peasants through London, capturing and beheading King Henry VI's associates, issues a manifesto of grievances.

JUNE 4, 1920 The republican-socialist Jangal movement forms the short-lived Persian Soviet Socialist State in the Gilan province of Iran. "By the will of the working people, Soviet power has been organized in Persia." —LETTER TO TROTSKY FROM THE REVOLUTIONARY WAR COUNCIL OF THE PERSIAN RED ARMY

JUNE 4, 1989 As army tanks roll into Beijing's Tiananmen Square, protestors join Hou Dejian in singing his popular song, "Heirs of the Dragon."

> "Enemies on all sides, the sword of the dictator.
> For how many years did those gunshots resound?"

JUNE 5, 1870 Jacob Riis immigrates to the US from Denmark, initially seeking employment as a carpenter but eventually becoming a pioneering photojournalist and New York City reformer. "I believe that the danger of such conditions as are fast growing up around us is greater for the very freedom which they mock." —HOW THE OTHER HALF LIVES

JUNE 5, 1940 Novelist and Yorkshire radical J. B. Priestley broadcasts his first "Postscript" radio series for the BBC, which drew audiences of up to 16 million listeners, and was soon cancelled for being too leftist. "Britain, which in the years immediately before this war was rapidly losing such democratic virtues as it possessed, is now being bombed and burned into democracy."

JUNE 5, 2013 The _Guardian_ publishes the first batch of government documents leaked by National Security Agency whistle-blower Edward Snowden.

WEDNESDAY JUNE 02

Lord Saye and Sele Brought Before Jake Cade 4th July 1450 by Charles Lucy

THURSDAY JUNE 03

NOTES:

FRIDAY JUNE 04

SATURDAY JUNE 05

SUNDAY JUNE 06

_____

_____

_____

_____

_____

_____

_____

_____

MONDAY JUNE 07

_____

_____

_____

_____

_____

_____

_____

TUESDAY JUNE 08

_____

_____

_____

_____

_____

_____

_____

JUNE 7, 1903 James Connolly founds the Socialist Labour Party with comrades in Edinburgh; he is later executed for his role in the Easter Uprising. "Before a shot has been fired by the British army on land, before a battle has been fought at sea, ruin and misery are entering the homes of the working people." —"WAR—WHAT IT MEANS TO YOU"

JUNE 10, 1952 Trinidadian historian, novelist and critic C.L.R. James is detained at Ellis Island to await deportation from the US. "The African bruises and breaks himself against his bars in the interests of freedoms wider than his own." —A HISTORY OF NEGRO REVOLT

JUNE 10, 1967 The June 1967 War between Israel and Syria, Jordan, and Egypt ends in Arab defeat.

"My grieved country,
In a flash
You changed me from a poet who wrote love poems
To a poet who writes with a knife."
—SYRIAN POET AND DIPLOMAT NIZAR QABBANI,
"FOOTNOTE TO THE BOOK OF SETBACK"

JUNE 12, 1917 Founding of the Liberty League, the first organization of the "New Negro Movement" by Hubert Harrison, a black intellectual and labor leader who immigrated to the US from the US Virgin Islands.

WEDNESDAY JUNE 09

Trinidadian historian, novelist and critic C.L.R. James

THURSDAY JUNE 10

NOTES:

FRIDAY JUNE 11

SATURDAY JUNE 12

SUNDAY JUNE 13

_____

_____

_____

_____

_____

_____

MONDAY JUNE 14

_____

_____

_____

_____

_____

_____

TUESDAY JUNE 15

_____

_____

_____

_____

_____

_____

JUNE 13, 1971 The _New York Times_ publishes the first of the Daniel Ellsberg–leaked Pentagon Papers, which proved that the US government misled the public on the Vietnam War. "If the war was unjust, as I now regarded it, that meant that every Vietnamese killed by Americans or by the proxies we had financed since the 1950s had been killed by us without justification." —_SECRETS: A MEMOIR OF VIETNAM AND THE PENTAGON PAPERS_

JUNE 15, 1813 Simón Bolívar issues his "Decree of War to the Death" for independence from Spain in Trujillo, Venezuela. "Spaniards and Canarians, count on death, even if indifferent, if you do not actively work in favor of the independence of America. Americans, count on life, even if guilty."

JUNE 16, 1948 The military arm of the Malayan Communist Party fires the first shots of an insurrection against British rule. "Imperialism wants to suppress our struggle for better living conditions with guns and knives and we must answer with more vigorous and larger-scale unified struggle." —EDITORIAL IN PARTY NEWSPAPER _MIN SHENG PAO_

JUNE 16, 1971 The Polynesian Panther Party is formed in Auckland as a Maori and Pacific Islander civil rights group.

JUNE 18, 1984 British police attack picketing miners with dogs, riot gear and armored vehicles, in a pivotal event of the 1984–85 UK Miners' Strike. The Battle of Orgreave is believed to be the first use of kettling, the police tactic of deploying a large cordon of officers to surround and entrap protesters.

WEDNESDAY JUNE 16

Polynesian Panther Party poster, c. 1973

THURSDAY JUNE 17

NOTES:

FRIDAY JUNE 18

SATURDAY JUNE 19

SUNDAY JUNE 20

_____

_____

_____

_____

_____

_____

MONDAY JUNE 21

_____

_____

_____

_____

_____

_____

_____

TUESDAY JUNE 22

_____

_____

_____

_____

_____

_____

_____

JUNE 22, 1955 Historian Eric Williams founds the People's National Movement, which later ushers in independence in Trinidad and Tobago. "The history of our West Indian islands can be expressed in two simple words: Columbus and Sugar." —CAPITALISM AND SLAVERY

JUNE 22, 1897 Indian anticolonialists shoot two British officers, and independence leader Bal Gangadhar Tilak is arrested for incitement. "Swaraj [self-rule] is my birthright and I shall have it!"

JUNE 25, 1876 Battle of Little Bighorn begins in what is now Montana, with combined Lakota, Cheyenne, and Arapaho forces beating the US 7th Cavalry. "I have robbed, killed, and injured too many white men to believe in a good peace. They are medicine, and I would eventually die a lingering death. I would rather die on the field of battle." —NATIVE LEADER SITTING BULL

JUNE 25, 1892 Ida B. Wells, civil rights activist and anti-lynching campaigner, publishes an early version of her pamphlet "Southern Horrors: Lynch Law in All Its Phases." "When the white man who is always the aggressor knows he runs as great a risk of biting the dust every time his Afro-American victim does, he will have greater respect for Afro-American life."

JUNE 25, 1962 Mozambique's anticolonial liberation party FRELIMO is founded. In the early 1970s, its guerrilla force of 7,000 fought 60,000 Portuguese colonial troops.

"In our land
bullets are beginning to flower."
—JORGE REBELO, POET BEHIND FRELIMO'S
PROPAGANDA CAMPAIGN

WEDNESDAY JUNE 23

Civil rights activst and suffragist Ida B. Wells (1862–1931)

THURSDAY JUNE 24

NOTES:

FRIDAY JUNE 25

SATURDAY JUNE 26

Make It Through by Roger Peet (Justseeds Artists Coop/justseeds.org)

NOW by Pete Railand (Justseeds Artists Coop/justseeds.org)

SUNDAY JUNE 27

_____

_____

_____

_____

_____

_____

_____

MONDAY JUNE 28

_____

_____

_____

_____

_____

_____

TUESDAY JUNE 29

_____

_____

_____

_____

_____

_____

JUNE 27, 1905 The Industrial Workers of the World is founded in Chicago, combining Marxist and trade unionist principles. "I believe we can agree that we should unite into one great organization—big enough to take in the children that are now working; big enough to take in the black man; big enough to take in all nationalities ..." —WILLIAM "BIG BILL" HAYWOOD, "THE GENERAL STRIKE"

JUNE 27, 1880 Helen Keller, world-renowned deafblind author and speaker, is born in Alabama. "If I ever contribute to the Socialist movement the book that I sometimes dream of, I know what I shall name it: Industrial Blindness and Social Deafness." —"HOW I BECAME A SOCIALIST"

JUNE 28, 1969 Riots begin at New York City's Stonewall Inn in response to a police raid, sparking the modern gay rights movement.

JUNE 30, 1840 Pierre-Joseph Proudhon, French revolutionary and first self-declared anarchist, publishes his _What Is Property?_ "Property is theft!"

JUNE 30, 1855 The Santhal Rebellion, led by two brothers, sees peasants across the Bengal Presidency rise up against the British Raj and local landlords.

JULY 2, 1809 Shawnee chief Tecumseh calls on all Indians to unite against the encroachment of white settlers on native land. "The only way to stop this evil is for all the red men to unite in claiming an equal right in the land. That is how it was at first, and should be still, for the land never was divided, but was for the use of everyone." —ADDRESS TO WILLIAM HENRY HARRISON

WEDNESDAY JUNE 30

_____
_____
_____
_____
_____
_____
_____

Marsha P. Johnson and Sylvia Rivera, prominent activists who led the Stonewall Riots

THURSDAY JULY 01

_____
_____
_____
_____
_____
_____
_____

NOTES:

_____
_____
_____
_____
_____

FRIDAY JULY 02

_____
_____
_____
_____
_____
_____
_____

SATURDAY JULY 03

_____
_____
_____
_____
_____
_____

SUNDAY JULY 04

_____

_____

_____

_____

_____

_____

_____

MONDAY JULY 05

_____

_____

_____

_____

_____

_____

_____

TUESDAY JULY 06

_____

_____

_____

_____

_____

_____

_____

JULY 4, 1789 The Marquis de Sade is moved from the Bastille prison to Charenton, days before French revolutionaries storm it and set fire to his writings there. "No act of possession can ever be perpetrated on a free being; it is as unjust to own a wife monogamously as it is to own slaves." —"PHILOSOPHY IN THE BEDROOM"

JULY 4, 1876 Susan B. Anthony and other protesters present the "Declaration of Rights for Women" at an official celebration of the centennial of the United States. "Women's wealth, thought, and labor have cemented the stones of every monument man has reared to liberty."

JULY 4, 1967 The British Parliament decriminalizes homosexuality.

JULY 5, 1885 The Protect the King movement in Vietnam begins, following a French attack on the imperial capital of Hue, and uniting the country against French colonial rule. "Better to be sentenced once than sentenced for eternity." —COORDINATOR OF RESISTANCE IN NORTHERN VIETNAM NGUYỄN QUANG BÍCH, LETTER TO THE FRENCH

JULY 7, 1969 Redstockings, a New York–based radical Marxist-feminist group, publishes its manifesto. "Liberated women—very different from women's liberation!" —REDSTOCKINGS MEMBER PAT MAINARDI, "THE POLITICS OF HOUSEWORK"

JULY 9, 1910 Govan Mbeki, leader of the South African Communist Party and the African National Congress, born. Following the Rivonia Trial, Mbeki served a long-term on Robben Island, during which he managed to run education classes with prisoners, many on Marxist theory, and wrote a number of significant analyses jail.

WEDNESDAY JULY 07

_____

_____

_____

_____

_____

_____

_____

Activists and supporters march outside the Rivonia Trial, 1964

THURSDAY JULY 08

_____

_____

_____

_____

_____

_____

_____

NOTES:

_____

_____

_____

_____

_____

_____

FRIDAY JULY 09

_____

_____

_____

_____

_____

_____

_____

SATURDAY JULY 10

_____

_____

_____

_____

_____

_____

SUNDAY JULY 11

_____

_____

_____

_____

_____

_____

_____

MONDAY JULY 12

_____

_____

_____

_____

_____

_____

_____

TUESDAY JULY 13

_____

_____

_____

_____

_____

_____

JULY 13, 1524 Thomas Müntzer, radical German theologian who became a leader in the Peasants' War of 1524 to 1525, delivers his famous "Sermon to the Princes" to Saxon nobles. "Oh, you beloved lords, how well the Lord will smash down the old pots of clay [ecclesiastical authorities] with his rod of iron."

JULY 13, 1934 Nobel Prize–winning Nigerian poet and playwright Wole Soyinka is born. Over the course of his life, Soyinka is prosecuted and jailed numerous times for his outspoken political critiques.

"Traveler you must set forth
At dawn.
I promise marvels of the holy hour."
—"DEATH IN THE DAWN"

JULY 14, 1789 An organized mob breaks into a royal armory in Paris and, newly armed, storms the Bastille, a fortress that held the monarchy's political prisoners. "This very night all the Swiss and German battalions will leave the Champ de Mars to massacre us all. One resource is left; to take arms!" —SPEECH BY JOURNALIST CAMILLE DESMOULINS THAT ROUSED THE PEOPLE THE PREVIOUS DAY

JULY 14, 1877 The Great Railroad Strike begins in West Virginia, United States, pitting thousands of railroad workers against state militias and the national guardsmen summoned to break it. "Wages and revenge." —SLOGAN

WEDNESDAY JULY 14

Blockade of engines at Martinsburg, West Virginia, 1877

THURSDAY JULY 15

NOTES:

FRIDAY JULY 16

SATURDAY JULY 17

SUNDAY JULY 18

MONDAY JULY 19

TUESDAY JULY 20

JULY 18, 1936 Resistance fighter Buenaventura Durruti forms the "Durruti Column," the largest anarchist fighting force in the Spanish Civil War. "The bourgeoisie might blast and ruin its own world before it leaves the stage of history. We carry a new world here, in our hearts." —DURRUTI IN AN INTERVIEW THREE MONTHS BEFORE BEING KILLED

JULY 19, 1961 The Sandinista National Liberation Front (FSLN) is founded; in 1979 it will overthrow the Somoza dictatorship in Nicaragua. "Those of us who propose to wage a struggle to liberate our country and make freedom a reality must rescue our own traditions and put together the facts and figures we need in order to wage an ideological war against our enemy." —FSLN COFOUNDER CARLOS FONSECA, SPEECH IN HAVANA

JULY 19, 1979 Ernesto Cardenal, Liberation Theology priest and poet aligned with the Sandinistas, becomes the first minister of culture under the new revolutionary government.

> "We shall celebrate in the great squares the anniversary of the Revolution
> The God that does exist is the god of the workers."
>
> —PSALM ("SALMO") 43

JULY 20, 1925 Frantz Fanon, psychiatrist and revolutionary whose writings inspired anticolonial movements throughout the world, is born in Martinique. "HISTORY teaches us clearly that the battle against colonialism does not run straight away along the lines of nationalism." —THE WRETCHED OF THE EARTH

JULY 23, 1900 W. E. B. Du Bois attends the First Pan-African Congress in London, where he makes the statement later immortalized in his 1903 book *Souls of Black Folk*: "The problem of the twentieth century is the problem of the color-line."

WEDNESDAY JULY 21

_____

_____

_____

_____

_____

_____

_____

W. E. B. Du Bois—American sociologist, historian, civil rights activist, Pan-Africanist, author and editor—in 1918

THURSDAY JULY 22

_____

_____

_____

_____

_____

_____

_____

NOTES:

_____

_____

_____

_____

_____

_____

FRIDAY JULY 23

_____

_____

_____

_____

_____

_____

_____

SATURDAY JULY 24

_____

_____

_____

_____

_____

_____

WHAT IS THE DIFFERENCE BETWEEN
VIOLENCE AND NONVIOLENCE?
JUDITH BUTLER

As much as it would make matters easier to
be able to identify violence in a way that is
clear and commands consensus, this proves
impossible to do in a political situation where
the power to attribute violence to the opposition itself becomes an instrument by which to
enhance state power, to discredit the aims of
the opposition, or even to justify their radical
disenfranchisement, imprisonment, and murder. At such moments, the attribution has to
be countered on the grounds that it is untrue
and unfair. But how is that to be done in a
public sphere where semantic confusion has
been sown about what is and is not violent?
Are we left with a confusing array of opinions
about violence and nonviolence and forced to
admit to a generalized relativism? Or can we
establish a way of distinguishing between a
tactical attribution of violence that falsifies and
inverts its direction, and those forms of violence, often structural and systemic, that too
often elude direct naming and apprehension?

If one wants to make an argument in favor of
nonviolence, it will be necessary to understand
and evaluate the ways that violence is figured
and attributed within a field of discursive, social,
and state power; the inversions that are tactically

performed; and the phantasmatic character of the attribution itself. Further, we will have to undertake a critique of the schemes by which state violence justifies itself, and the relation of those justificatory schemes to the effort to maintain its monopoly on violence. That monopoly depends upon a naming practice, one that often dissimulates violence as legal coercion or externalizes its own violence onto its target, rediscovering it as the violence of the other.

To argue for or against nonviolence requires that we establish the difference between violence and nonviolence, if we can. But there is no quick way to arrive at a stable semantic distinction between the two when that distinction is so often exploited for the purposes of concealing and extending violent aims and practices. In other words, we cannot race to the phenomenon itself without passing through the conceptual schemes that dispose the use of the term in various directions, and without an analysis of how those dispositions work. If those accused of doing violence while engaging in no violent acts seek to dispute the status of the accusation as unjustifiable, they will have to demonstrate how the allegation of violence is used—not just "what it says," but "what it is doing with what is said." Within what episteme does it gather credibility? In other words, why is it sometimes believed, and most crucially, what can be done to expose and defeat the effective character of the speech act—its plausibility effect?

To start down such a path, we have to accept that "violence" and "nonviolence" are used variably and perversely, without pitching into a form of nihilism suffused by the belief that violence and nonviolence are whatever those in power decide they should be. Part of the task of this book is to accept the difficulty of finding and securing the definition of violence when it is subject to instrumental definitions that serve political interests and sometimes state violence itself. In my view, that difficulty does not imply a chaotic relativism that would undermine the task of critical thought in order to expose an instrumental use of that distinction that is both false and harmful. Both violence and nonviolence arrive in the fields of moral debate and political analysis already interpreted, worked over by prior usages. There is no way to avoid the demand to interpret both violence and nonviolence, and to assess the distinction between them, if we hope to oppose state violence and to reflect carefully on the justifiability of violent tactics on the left. As we wade into moral philosophy here, we find ourselves in the crosscurrents where moral and political philosophy meet, with consequences for both how we end up doing politics, and what world we seek to help bring into being.

This is a revised extract from The Force of Nonviolence: An Ethico-Political Bind *by Judith Butler (Verso, 2020).*

SUNDAY JULY 25

_____

_____

_____

_____

_____

_____

MONDAY JULY 26

_____

_____

_____

_____

_____

_____

_____

TUESDAY JULY 27

_____

_____

_____

_____

_____

_____

JULY 25, 1846 Henry David Thoreau is jailed for refusing to pay taxes due to his opposition to slavery and the Mexican-American war. "Under a government which imprisons any unjustly, the true place for a just man is also a prison." —*CIVIL DISOBEDIENCE*

JULY 26, 1953 Fidel Castro leads the Cuban revolution against the US-backed dictator Fulgencio Batista with an attack on the Moncada Barracks. "Condemn me. It does not matter. History will absolve me." —CASTRO, BEFORE BEING SENTENCED FOR THE ATTACK

JULY 26, 1956 Gamal Abdel Nasser, president of Egypt, announces the nationalization of the Suez Canal. "We shall yield neither to force nor the dollar."

JULY 27, 1972 Selma James, cofounder of the International Wages for Housework campaign, and Mariarosa Dalla Costa publish *The Power of Women and the Subversion of the Community*, which identified women's unwaged care work as an essential element of capitalism. "We must refuse housework as women's work, as work imposed upon us, which we never invented, which has never been paid for, in which they have forced us to cope with absurd hours, twelve and thirteen a day, in order to force us to stay at home."

JULY 28, 1794 Maximilien Robespierre, the face of the French Revolution's Reign of Terror, is guillotined without a trial. "The tyrant's trial is insurrection; his judgment is the fall of his power; his penalty, whatever the liberty of the people demands." —"AGAINST GRANTING THE KING A TRIAL"

JULY 29, 1848 The Young Irelander Rebellion of 1848 takes place: a failed Irish nationalist revolt against British rule, sometimes called the Famine Rebellion (since it took place during the Great Irish Famine) or the Battle of Ballingarry.

WEDNESDAY JULY 28

Castro with fellow revolutionary Camilo Cienfuegos entering
Havana, 1959

THURSDAY JULY 29

NOTES:

FRIDAY JULY 30

SATURDAY JULY 31

SUNDAY AUGUST 01

AUGUST 1, 1933 Anti-Fascist activists Bruno Tesch, Walter Möller, Karl Wolff and August Lütgens executed by the Nazi regime in Altona.

AUGUST 2, 1924 James Baldwin, black American novelist, critic, and essayist, is born in Harlem, New York City. "People can cry much easier than they can change, a rule of psychology people like me picked up as kids on the street." —"JAMES BALDWIN BACK HOME"

AUGUST 3, 1960 Independence Day in the Republic of Niger, marking the nation's independence from France in 1960. Since 1975, it is also Arbor Day, as trees are planted across the nation to aid the fight against desertification.

MONDAY AUGUST 02

AUGUST 4, 1983 Revolutionary leader Thomas Sankara assumes power in Burkina Faso, nationalizing mineral wealth and redistributing land. "It took the madmen of yesterday for us to be able to act with extreme clarity today. I want to be one of those madmen. We must dare to invent the future."

AUGUST 5, 1951 Eduardo Chibas, anti-communist Cuban radio personality, shoots himself after his final broadcast. "People of Cuba, keep awake. This is my last knock at your door." —CHIBAS'S LAST WORDS

TUESDAY AUGUST 03

AUGUST 6, 1969 Theodor Adorno—philosopher, composer and leading member of the Frankfurt School of critical theory—dies. "For the Enlightenment, anything which cannot be resolved into numbers, and ultimately into one, is illusion; modern positivism consigns it to poetry." —DIALECTIC OF ENLIGHTENMENT, CO-AUTHORED WITH MAX HORKHEIMER

AUGUST 6, 2011 Riots break out throughout London after police kill a black man, lasting for several days and leading to more than 3,000 arrests.

WEDNESDAY AUGUST 04

Writer and critic James Baldwin (1924–1987)

THURSDAY AUGUST 05

NOTES:

FRIDAY AUGUST 06

SATURDAY AUGUST 07

SUNDAY AUGUST 08

_____

_____

_____

_____

_____

_____

_____

_____

MONDAY AUGUST 09

_____

_____

_____

_____

_____

_____

TUESDAY AUGUST 10

_____

_____

_____

_____

_____

_____

_____

AUGUST 8, 1961 Wu Han, a member of a dissident group of Chinese intellectuals, writes a play indirectly critical of Mao and the Great Leap Forward, for which he is imprisoned.

> "You pay lip service to the principle
> that the people are the roots of the state.
> But officials still oppress the masses
> while pretending to be virtuous men."
> —"HAI JUI'S DISMISSAL"

AUGUST 8, 1988 Rangoon students call openly for democracy, sparking the 8888 Uprising that toppled Burma's Ne Win government before being violently crushed by government troops.

AUGUST 9, 1650 The English Parliament passes an act outlawing "blasphemous" sects like the Ranters, one of the most radical to emerge during the English Revolution, which denied the authority of churches, priests, and writ.

AUGUST 11, 1828 The first Working Men's Party of the United States is founded in Philadelphia. "And for the support of this declaration, we mutually pledge to each other our faithful aid to the end of our lives." —GEORGE HENRY EVANS, "PARTY DECLARATION OF INDEPENDENCE"

AUGUST 14, 1980 Polish shipyard workers strike to protest the firing of worker Anna Walentynowicz and for the right to form unions. Walentynowicz is reinstated, and several weeks later, the first independent labor union in a Soviet bloc country, Solidarność, is formed, precipitating the fall of the Polish communist regime. "It was the end of the utopian dream, and it enabled us to dismantle the dictatorship by negotiation." —ACTIVIST ADAM MICHNIK

WEDNESDAY AUGUST 11

_____

_____

_____

_____

_____

_____

_____

THURSDAY AUGUST 12

_____

_____

_____

_____

_____

_____

FRIDAY AUGUST 13

_____

_____

_____

_____

_____

_____

_____

NOTES:

_____

_____

_____

_____

_____

_____

_____

_____

_____

_____

_____

_____

_____

SATURDAY AUGUST 14

_____

_____

_____

_____

_____

_____

_____

SUNDAY AUGUST 15

_____

_____

_____

_____

_____

_____

MONDAY AUGUST 16

_____

_____

_____

_____

_____

_____

_____

TUESDAY AUGUST 17

_____

_____

_____

_____

_____

_____

_____

AUGUST 15, 1947 India becomes independent after 200 years of British colonial rule. "A moment comes, which comes but rarely in history, when we step out from the old to the new, when an age ends, and when the soul of a nation, long suppressed, finds utterance." —MOVEMENT LEADER AND INDIA'S FIRST PRIME MINISTER JAWAHARLAL NEHRU, "TRYST WITH DESTINY"

AUGUST 16, 1819 The English cavalry charges into a crowd of over 60,000 rallying in Manchester for parliamentary reform in what becomes known as the Peterloo Massacre.

"Rise like lions after slumber
In unvanquishable number!
Shake your chains to earth like dew
Which in sleep had fallen on you:
Ye are many—they are few!"

—PERCY BYSSHE SHELLEY'S "THE MASQUE OF ANARCHY," AN EARLY STATEMENT OF NONVIOLENT RESISTANCE

AUGUST 21, 1791 A rebellion against slavery breaks out in Saint Domingue, leading to the Haitian Revolution, the only slave revolt against European colonialists that successfully achieved an independent state. "We seek only to bring men to the liberty that God has given them, and that other men have taken from them only by transgressing His immutable will." —REVOLUTIONARY LEADER TOUSSAINT L'OUVERTURE

AUGUST 21, 1940 Leon Trotsky, Marxist revolutionary and theorist, is assassinated by Soviet agents. "Life is beautiful. Let the future generations cleanse it of all evil, oppression and violence, and enjoy it to the full." —"TROTSKY'S TESTAMENT," WRITTEN MONTHS EARLIER

WEDNESDAY AUGUST 18

_____

_____

_____

_____

_____

_____

_____

A painting of the Peterloo Massacre circulated in pro-suffrage papers, 1819

THURSDAY AUGUST 19

_____

_____

_____

_____

_____

_____

_____

NOTES:

_____

_____

_____

_____

_____

_____

FRIDAY AUGUST 20

_____

_____

_____

_____

_____

_____

_____

SATURDAY AUGUST 21

_____

_____

_____

_____

_____

_____

_____

SUNDAY AUGUST 22

MONDAY AUGUST 23

TUESDAY AUGUST 24

AUGUST 23, 1572 French Catholics, incited by the monarchy, kill thousands of Protestants (known as Huguenots) in the St. Bartholomew's Day Massacre, giving rise to the Monarchomachs, a movement supporting tyrannicide.

AUGUST 23, 1927 During the Red Scare—a period of intense political repression in the US—the Italian-born anarchists Nicola Sacco and Bartolomeo Vanzetti are wrongfully convicted and executed for robbery and murder.

AUGUST 25, 1968 Yippies—the Youth International Party, which brought counterculture theatricality to the US antiwar and New Left movements—host their Festival of Life at the Democratic National Convention in Chicago, leading to police actions and a trial for conspiracy to riot for the organizers. "There will be public fornication whenever and wherever there is an aroused appendage and willing apertures." —ACTIVIST ED SANDERS, "PREDICTIONS FOR YIPPIE ACTIVITIES"

AUGUST 26 1789 The "Declaration of the Rights of Man and of the Citizen"—a document of the French Revolution and civil rights—is adopted by the National Constituent Assembly in France. Nicolas de Condorcet, Etta Palm d'Aelders and Olympe de Gouges called for these rights to be extended to women; Vincent Ogé, followed by the Haitian Revolution of 1791-1804, attempted to extend them to men of color and then to slaves.

WEDNESDAY AUGUST 25

Declaration of the Rights of Man and of the Citizen, painted by Jean-Jacques-François Le Barbier

THURSDAY AUGUST 26

NOTES:

FRIDAY AUGUST 27

SATURDAY AUGUST 28

FRIENDSHIP AS A WAY OF LIFE
LESLIE KERN

In *Notes from a Feminist Killjoy*, literature scholar Erin Wunker explores female friendships as sustaining and transformational. She asks a provocative question: "What would female friendship as a way of life look like?" Work highlighting the complexity of female friendship is much rarer than movies, television shows, and books that gloss over women's friendships to focus instead on romantic relationships, family lives, and dramatic life events. Friendship is relegated to the background as a simple plot or character device for moving the real action along. Wunker wonders what might be possible if we resist "representations of female friendships that police those friendships into invisibility or strip them of their radical potential?" I wonder, what ways of being in the city are lost or ignored when we view female friendships as frivolous and disposable?

The phrase "female friendship as a way of life" resonates with me so deeply. Although my adult life has involved a strong commitment to my career, raising a child, marriage, divorce, and various romantic attachments as well as moving to another province, my friendships with other women have been the stable, consistent core and sometimes even

the highest priority amongst a range of competing demands. My two main "girl gangs" have made me who I am and I couldn't imagine giving them up. One of them has endured for the better part of twenty-five years now, longer than any relationship and pre-dating parenthood and career. When I picture retirement, it's their faces I see around me. Wunker herself reflects on the constellation of support, knowledge, care, and loving critique she's received from her friendships and describes friendships among women as "worldmaking." In queer theory, worldmaking includes creative, disruptive, utopian, and even failed performances, practices, relationships, and imaginings that not only challenge structures like hetero- and homonormativity, public and private, etc., but that map queer, insurgent, other worlds beyond the already charted pathways. Worldmaking means the process of both imagining and creating space(s) where things can unfold otherwise. Practicing female friendship as a way of life is, I think, a worldmaking activity.

Too often, women's friendships are misunderstood as second-rate substitutions for romantic heterosexual relationships or veiled lesbian love. Certainly, there's a long, often hidden history of women's friendships as masks for actual lesbian relationships that couldn't be publicly acknowledged. Even when lesbianism isn't the subtext, close female friendships might be viewed as substitutes for romantic partnership or as supplying something that romantic partners (especially male romantic partners) cannot. Wunker worries that "recycling one storyline—the romance—means dragging all the sedimented associations of that storyline with you." It seems that culturally we lack a language to adequately describe the character and quality of female friendships without resorting to borrowed vocabulary or miscategorizations.

Even more problematically, popular representations swing between the stereotype of the bitchy, jealous, always-on-the-verge-of-a-catfight friendship and the overly mythologized, fraught, mysterious, and unknowable friendship. Wunker describes the latter as creating a "dense, atmospheric pressure surrounding discourses of female friendship." In her bestselling essay collection *Bad Feminist*, Roxane Gay implores readers to "abandon the cultural myth that all female friendships must be bitchy, toxic or competitive. This myth is like heels and purses—pretty but designed to SLOW women down." Gay lays down thirteen rules for female friendships, designed to tear down the damaging myths that put walls between us and constantly undermine our attempts at connection. As she notes in rule number one, these myths are designed to slow women down: they keep us locked in competition, holding one another at arm's length out of fear, jealousy, or insecurity. They keep us from joining forces and realizing the power of friendship for transforming our worlds and ourselves.

This is a revised extract from Feminist City: Claiming Space in a Man-Made World *by Leslie Kern (Verso, 2020).*

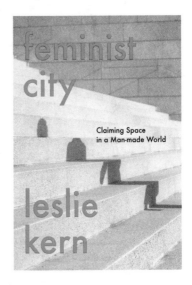

SUNDAY AUGUST 29

MONDAY AUGUST 30

TUESDAY AUGUST 31

AUGUST 29, 1786 Poor farmers crushed by debt and taxes rise up in armed rebellion in Massachusetts, US, in what came to be known as Shay's Rebellion. "The great men are going to get all we have and I think it is time for us to rise and put a stop to it, and have no more courts, nor sheriffs, nor collectors, nor lawyers." —PLOUGH JOGGER, FARMER, SPEAKING AT THE ILLEGAL CONVENTION OPPOSING THE MASSACHUSETTS LEGISLATURE

AUGUST 29, 1844 Edward Carpenter, pioneering socialist poet, philosopher, and early homosexual thinker, is born in England. "It has become clear that the number of individuals affected with 'sexual inversion' in some degree or other is very great—much greater than is generally supposed to be the case." —HOMOGENIC LOVE

SEPTEMBER 1, 1961 The Eritrean struggle for independence begins when members of the Eritrean Liberation Front fire first shots on the occupying Ethiopian army.

"What have I done
That you deny me my torch?"
    —"SHIGEY HABUNI," POPULAR SONG WITH TIES TO
    THE NATIONALIST MOVEMENT

SEPTEMBER 3, 2017 Private security guards for the Dakota Access Pipeline unleash dogs on indigenous water protectors near the Standing Rock Sioux Tribe reservation in North Dakota. A protest encampment, established months earlier, quickly swelled to become the largest gathering of Native Americans in recent history. "Mní Wičoni—Water is Life." —SLOGAN

WEDNESDAY SEPTEMBER 01

Standing Rock Sioux Tribe reservation logo, 1873

THURSDAY SEPTEMBER 02

NOTES:

FRIDAY SEPTEMBER 03

SATURDAY SEPTEMBER 04

SUNDAY SEPTEMBER 05

MONDAY SEPTEMBER 06

TUESDAY SEPTEMBER 07

SEPTEMBER 6, 1960 "Manifesto of the 121" is signed by French intellectuals (including Jean-Paul Sartre, Maurice Blanchot, and others), supporting the right of Algerians to fight for independence from the French. "Must we be reminded that fifteen years after the destruction of the Hitlerite order, French militarism has managed to bring back torture and restore it as an institution in Europe?"

SEPTEMBER 7, 1872 Russian revolutionary and anarchist theorist Mikhail Bakunin is expelled from the First International, presaging a split between the anarchist and Marxist factions of the workers' movement. "If you took the most ardent revolutionary, vested him in absolute power, within a year he would be worse than the Tsar himself."
—BAKUNIN ON AUTHORITARIAN SOCIALISM

SEPTEMBER 8, 1965 Delano Grape Strike begins in California when Filipino grape pickers walk out and ask Cesar Chavez, leader of the mostly Latino National Farm Workers Association, to join them. The campaign ended five years later in success, largely due to a consumer boycott. "Time accomplishes for the poor what money does for the rich." —CHAVEZ, "LETTER FROM DELANO"

SEPTEMBER 9, 869 Ali ibn Muhammad, a leader of the Zanj uprising of African slaves against the Abbasid Caliphate in Iraq, begins freeing slaves and gaining adherents. "Ali ordered their slaves to bring whips of palm branches and, while their masters and agents were prostrated on the ground, each one was given five hundred lashes." —PERSIAN HISTORIAN IBN JARIR AL-TABARI

SEPTEMBER 9, 1739 Stono Rebellion, the largest slave uprising in Britain's mainland North American colonies, led by a slave called Jemmy, erupts near Charleston, South Carolina. Over the next two years, slave uprisings occurred independently in Georgia and South Carolina, inspired by the Stono Rebellion.

WEDNESDAY SEPTEMBER 08

Cesar Chavez (1927–1993) following the successful farmworker strike and consumer grape boycott, 1970

THURSDAY SEPTEMBER 09

NOTES:

FRIDAY SEPTEMBER 10

SATURDAY SEPTEMBER 11

SUNDAY SEPTEMBER 12

_____

_____

_____

_____

_____

_____

_____

MONDAY SEPTEMBER 13

_____

_____

_____

_____

_____

_____

TUESDAY SEPTEMBER 14

_____

_____

_____

_____

_____

_____

SEPTEMBER 14, 1791 Olympe de Gouges publishes the _Declaration of the Rights of Women and the Female Citizen,_ one of the first tracts to champion women's rights. "Woman is born free and remains the equal of man in rights."

SEPTEMBER 15, 1889 Claude McKay, Harlem Renaissance poet and delegate to the Third International, is born in Jamaica.

"If we must die—O let us nobly die!
So that our precious blood may not be shed
In vain; then even the monsters we defy
Shall be constrained to honor us though
dead!"

—"IF WE MUST DIE"

SEPTEMBER 16, 1810 Miguel Hidalgo, a priest in Dolores, Mexico, issues a call to revolt against Spanish rule, setting in motion the Mexican War of Independence. "My children: a new dispensation come to us today. Will you receive it? Will you free yourselves?"

SEPTEMBER 16, 1923 Alongside her lover and his six-year-old nephew, Ito Noe, anarchist and feminist writer and activist, is brutally murdered by Japanese police. The event, known as the Amakasu Incident, sparked outrage throughout Japan and led to a ten-year sentence for the officer.

SEPTEMBER 16, 1973 Victor Jara, Chilean poet and songwriter, is tortured and killed in Chile Stadium following Pinochet's coup against Allende.

"How hard is it to sing
when I must sing of horror"

—"ESTADIO CHILE," WRITTEN BY JARA IN THE STADIUM
AND SMUGGLED OUT INSIDE A SHOE

WEDNESDAY SEPTEMBER 15

Ito Noe, Japanese anarchist and feminist

THURSDAY SEPTEMBER 16

NOTES:

FRIDAY SEPTEMBER 17

SATURDAY SEPTEMBER 18

SUNDAY SEPTEMBER 19

MONDAY SEPTEMBER 20

TUESDAY SEPTEMBER 21

SEPTEMBER 19, 1921 The Brazilian educator and philosopher Paulo Freire is born. His *Pedagogy of the Oppressed* infuses a classical theory of education with Marxist and anticolonialist approaches. "This, then, is the great humanistic and historical task of the oppressed: to liberate themselves and their oppressors as well."

SEPTEMBER 21, 1956 Nicaraguan poet Rigoberto López Pérez assassinates Anastasio Somoza García, the longtime dictator of Nicaragua, before being killed himself. "Seeing that all efforts to return Nicaragua to being (or to becoming for the first time) a free country without shame or stain have been futile, I have decided that I should be the one to try to initiate the beginning of the end of this tyranny." —LETTER TO HIS MOTHER

SEPTEMBER 23, 1884 Liberal party partisans occupy a mountaintop in Kabasan, Japan, in a rebellion against the Meiji government.

"Yet while we lament, asking
why our insignificant selves
were oppressed,
the rain still falls
heavily on the people."
—PARTICIPANT OHASHI GENZABURO

SEPTEMBER 24, 1838 A meeting held on Kersal Moor in England launches the Chartist movement, the first mass working-class movement in Europe.
—THE PEOPLE'S CHARTER AND PETITION

WEDNESDAY SEPTEMBER 22

Great Chartist Meeting on Kennington Common, London in 1848

THURSDAY SEPTEMBER 23

NOTES:

FRIDAY SEPTEMBER 24

SATURDAY SEPTEMBER 25

All We Have Is Each Other by N.O. Bonzo

Global Climate Strike by Aaron Hughes (Justseeds Artists Coop/justseeds.org)

SUNDAY SEPTEMBER 26

SEPTEMBER 26, 1940 Fleeing Vichy France, Marxist theorist Walter Benjamin is threatened with deportation from Spain and kills himself with morphine tablets.

SEPTEMBER 28, 1829 David Walker, a contributor to the first African-American newspaper *Freedom Journal*, publishes his "Appeal to the Colored Citizens of the World," calling for slaves to revolt against their masters. Southern plantation owners respond by putting a $3,000 bounty on his head. "The whites want slaves, and want us for their slaves, but some of them will curse the day they ever saw us."

MONDAY SEPTEMBER 27

SEPTEMBER 1875 Senator William Allison arrives in Sioux country to negotiate a land lease agreement with the Native Americans that would have allowed the United States government to mine the area for gold. His proposal is met with 300 mounted warriors, led by Little Big Man, who chant the song below in response.

> "The Black Hills is my land and I love it
> And whoever interferes
> Will hear this gun."
> —SIOUX WARRIORS' SONG

SEPTEMBER 30, 1935 The anti-Stalinist Workers' Party of Marxist Unification (POUM) is founded in Spain, where it is especially active during the Civil War. "The totalitarian states can do great things, but there is one thing they cannot do: they cannot give the factory-worker a rifle and tell him to take it home and keep it in his bedroom. That rifle hanging on the wall of the working-class flat or laborer's cottage is the symbol of democracy."
—POUM MEMBER GEORGE ORWELL, ARTICLE IN THE *EVENING STANDARD*

TUESDAY SEPTEMBER 28

WEDNESDAY SEPTEMBER 29

Little Big Man—an Oglala Lakota, or Oglala Sioux, leader

THURSDAY SEPTEMBER 30

NOTES:

FRIDAY OCTOBER 01

SATURDAY OCTOBER 02

SUNDAY OCTOBER 03

_____

_____

_____

_____

_____

_____

_____

_____

MONDAY OCTOBER 04

_____

_____

_____

_____

_____

_____

_____

TUESDAY OCTOBER 05

_____

_____

_____

_____

_____

_____

_____

OCTOBER 5, 1877 Nez Perce leader Hinmatóowy-alahtq'it, also known as Chief Joseph, ends a legendary three-month flight to Canada by surrendering to US forces. "Do not misunderstand me, but understand fully with reference to my affection for the land. I never said the land was mine to do with as I choose. The one who has a right to dispose of it is the one who created it." —"AN INDIAN'S VIEW OF INDIAN AFFAIRS"

OCTOBER 5, 1959 Robert F. Williams's Black Armed Guard fires on Ku Klux Klan members riding past a member's house in North Carolina. "Nowhere in the annals of history does the record show a people delivered from bondage by patience alone." —"WE MUST FIGHT BACK"

OCTOBER 6, 1985 Riots break out on the Broadwater Farm estate in one of London's poorest neighborhoods, a day after an Afro-Caribbean woman died of heart failure during a police search. One police officer was killed.

OCTOBER 7, 1979 Landless farmers occupy the Macali land in Ronda Alta, Brazil, leading to the founding of the Landless Workers Movement (MST). "This is what I've always wanted: 'to overcome, to overcome.'" —MST LEADER MIGUEL ALVES DOS SANTOS

OCTOBER 8, 1969 The Weather Underground, a faction of the Students for a Democratic Society, stages the first of its "Days of Rage," a series of confrontations with the Chicago police in 1969. "Freaks are revolutionaries and revolutionaries are freaks. If you want to find us, this is where we are." —"COMMUNIQUÉ #1"

FBI "Wanted" poster for civil rights activist Robert F. Williams (1925-1996)

NOTES:

SUNDAY OCTOBER 10

_____

_____

_____

_____

_____

_____

_____

MONDAY OCTOBER 11

_____

_____

_____

_____

_____

_____

TUESDAY OCTOBER 12

_____

_____

_____

_____

_____

_____

_____

OCTOBER 10, 1903 British activist Emmeline Pankhurst cofounds the Women's Social and Political Union, a militant all-women suffragist organization dedicated to "deeds, not words." "The moving spirit of militancy is deep and abiding reverence for human life." —MY OWN STORY

OCTOBER 10, 1911 The Wuchang Uprising begins after the Qing government suppresses political protest against the handover of local railways to foreign ventures. Quickly spreading through China, the Xinhai Revolution took down the 2,100-year-old dynastic empire within months.

OCTOBER 10, 1947 Senegalese railway workers begin a strike that lasted months, in what would become a watershed moment in Senegal's anticolonial struggle. "It rolled out over its own length, like the movement of a serpent. It was as long as a life." —GOD'S BITS OF WOOD, A NOVEL BY FILMMAKER, WRITER, AND ACTIVIST OUSMANE SEMBÈNE BASED ON THE STRIKE

OCTOBER 15, 1966 The Black Panther Party is founded in Oakland, California. "The people make revolution; the oppressors, by their brutal actions, cause resistance by the people. The vanguard party only teaches the correct methods of resistance." —COFOUNDER HUEY P. NEWTON, "THE CORRECT HANDLING OF A REVOLUTION"

OCTOBER 15, 1968 The Jamaican government bans the Guyanese scholar and Black Power activist Walter Rodney from the country, sparking what became known as the Rodney Riots. "The only great men among the unfree and the oppressed are those who struggle to destroy the oppressor." —HOW EUROPE UNDERDEVELOPED AFRICA

WEDNESDAY OCTOBER 13

Black Panthers demonstrating outside of the Washington State
Capitol Building, 1969

THURSDAY OCTOBER 14

NOTES:

FRIDAY OCTOBER 15

SATURDAY OCTOBER 16

SUNDAY OCTOBER 17

_____

_____

_____

_____

_____

_____

_____

MONDAY OCTOBER 18

_____

_____

_____

_____

_____

_____

TUESDAY OCTOBER 19

_____

_____

_____

_____

_____

_____

OCTOBER 17, 1961 Algerian demonstrators in Paris, denouncing France's colonial war in their home country, are met with force. An estimated 300 were massacred; the French government acknowledges forty victims.

OCTOBER 18, 1899 The Battle of Senluo Temple breaks out in northern China between government forces and the Militia United in Righteousness—known in English as the "Boxers" for their strict martial arts regimen—in what would eventually become the Boxer Rebellion, an anti-foreign and anti-Christian uprising.

> "When at last all the Foreign Devils
> are expelled to the very last man,
> The Great Qing, united, together,
> will bring peace to this our land"
> —BOXERS WALL POSTER

OCTOBER 21, 1956 Dedan Kimathi, leader of Kenya's Mau Mau Uprising, is captured by a British colonial officer later nicknamed the "Butcher of Bahrain." "I lead them because God never created any nation to be ruled by another nation forever."

OCTOBER 22, 1964 Jean-Paul Sartre refuses to accept the Nobel Prize for Literature. "The writer must therefore refuse to let himself be transformed into an institution." —LETTER TO THE NOBEL COMMITTEE

OCTOBER 23, 1850 First National Women's Rights Convention meets in Worcester, Massachusetts. The following year, poet and journalist Elizabeth Oakes Smith is nominated as its president, only to be rejected after showing up in a dress baring her neck and arms. "Do we fully understand that we aim at nothing less than an entire subversion of the existing order of society, a dissolution of the whole existing social compact?"

WEDNESDAY OCTOBER 20

Elizabeth Oakes Smith (1806–1893), c. 1845, by John Wesley Paradise

THURSDAY OCTOBER 21

NOTES:

FRIDAY OCTOBER 22

SATURDAY OCTOBER 23

V

SHE CONTINUES TO THINK
JENNY HVAL

Let's see ... We're in a room, I think, a non-descript room. At this point it could be any room. It's still without depth, width, length or any sense of time ... It might have other dimensions, ones we don't yet know about, dimensions that don't have names. Perhaps we're in a room with a closed centre. There, at its core, it reserves space for something else. Everything else. Maybe a room without us has room for the connections between us.

From a distance we hear voices belonging to a class of teenage girls. The murmur comes from a cold classroom at the end of the hall. We glide between the girls into the classroom, invisible, like a video camera, while they recite their names one by one. They seem to have short and simple names, but we can't hear them, only an indistinct hum. It sounds as if we're outside the room, or as if we've stopped our ears with cotton and can only hear the drone from our own heads. We have to read their lips to understand what they're saying. A girl fills the frame and introduces

herself in two syllables. We can only see her lips. Maybe her name is Venke. As she says her name, icy mist escapes the corners of her mouth. Threads and bubbles of spit knot her lips together as she opens and closes them around two syllables. A weak shimmer that resembles a muted laptop gleam is coming from deep down in the girl's throat. The light escapes her mouth, filtered by her tongue and the different constellations of her teeth.

There are no windows, no bookshelves, no books, no coat racks or chalkboards around the girls. Instead, images are projected onto the spotless white concrete walls as if they were a canvas. Images of windows are projected onto the walls, with trees swaying in the wind, and images of bookshelves full of books on maths, geography, history, chemistry, Norwegian and Christianity. If it weren't for the concrete's rough surface, it might look almost real. Their school uniforms look almost real, too. They are wearing black, slightly stiff-looking

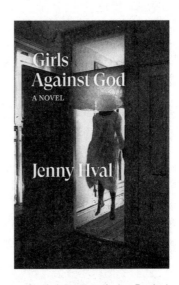

jackets with shoulder pads, and matching pleated skirts, but with yellow neon stripes on their sleeves and trainers. They look like a futurist marching band.

A teacher takes attendance from behind a desk at the far end of the room. She is wearing a fitted black suit with stripes that gradually shade from red to purple to blue. She yawns a little. Each time a girl says her name, this teacher taps a screen with her right index finger. As she takes their names she also sticks each finger of her left hand into a small machine that resembles an automatic pencil sharpener. The machine sands her nails neatly and paints them a gorgeous bright pink.

We continue to watch the girls' lips move. The murmur of voices and the hum from the air conditioning makes it impossible to discern individual words, but the conversation seems academic. Some lips are more energetic, they expel longer words from their mouths, working harder and producing more saliva. Other lips are softer and more questioning. Eyeshadow glitter falls on a shoulder, someone's chest, a desk; the glitter intermingles with the glare from the overhead lights.

There's a girl seated at the back of the classroom who's not quite paying attention. Everything she's wearing that isn't part of her uniform—her socks, undershirt, pants, bra—is black. She looks up from her writing. At first glance she seems to be writing in a notebook, but it's soon revealed to be a tablet. A small projector shaped like a gaping goat's head is attached to it. Light spills from the goat's mouth as if from a fountain and projects a 3D drawing of lines, text, and images onto the surface of the tablet.

The girl uses a pen to write in her book, then pushes the pen against the projection: the text disappears. She continues to think.

This is a revised extract from Girls Against God *by Jenny Hval (translated by Marjam Idriss, Verso, 2020).*

SUNDAY OCTOBER 24

MONDAY OCTOBER 25

TUESDAY OCTOBER 26

OCTOBER 27, 1967 The 1967 Abortion Act was passed in the United Kingdom, legalizing abortions for up to 28 weeks. Women in Northern Ireland continue to be excluded from access to this healthcare in their own country.

OCTOBER 28, 1647 The Putney Debates begin, in which members of the New Model Army, who had recently seized London, debate Britain's new constitution. "The poorest man in England is not bound in a strict sense to that government that he hath not had a voice to put himself under." —LEVELLERS SUPPORTER COLONEL RAINSBOROUGH ARGUING FOR UNIVERSAL MALE SUFFRAGE

OCTOBER 29, 1888 Li Dazhao, librarian, intellectual, and cofounder of the Chinese Communist Party, is born. "China is a rural nation and most of the laboring class consists of peasants. Unless they are liberated, our whole nation will not be liberated." —"DEVELOP THE PEASANTRY"

OCTOBER 29, 1956 Israel invades Egypt after its nationalization of the Suez Canal, followed a few days later by UK and French troops; they are met with local resistance.

"Not through hope will the prize be taken,
The world is taken by struggle."
    —THE "DIVA OF THE EAST" UMM KULTHUM'S POPULAR
    SONG "EGYPT SPEAKS OF HERSELF," WHICH COULD BE
    HEARD RINGING THROUGH THE STREETS

OCTOBER 30, 1969 The Kenya People's Union is banned, transforming the country into a one-party state; its leader, the Luo chief and first vice president of independent Kenya Oginga Odinga, is detained. "We fought for *uhuru* so that people may rule themselves. Direct action, not underhand diplomacy and silent intrigue by professional politicians, won *uhuru*, and only popular mobilization can make it meaningful." —*NOT YET UHURU*

WEDNESDAY OCTOBER 27

Chinese comintern Li Dazhao (1888-1927)

THURSDAY OCTOBER 28

NOTES:

FRIDAY OCTOBER 29

SATURDAY OCTOBER 30

SUNDAY OCTOBER 31

OCTOBER 31, 1517 Martin Luther composes his letter to the Catholic Church, the *95 Theses*, which quickly spread across Europe and spark the Protestant Reformation. "He who sees a man in need, and passes him by, and gives [his money] for pardons, purchases not the indulgences of the pope, but the indignation of God."

NOVEMBER 1811 A letter sent from "Ned Ludd" in Nottingham, England, threatens to break the looms of a property owner, in an early document from the Luddite Uprising.

"The guilty may fear but no vengeance he aims
At the honest man's life or Estate"
—LUDDITES, "GENERAL LUDDS TRIUMPH"

MONDAY NOVEMBER 01

NOVEMBER 1, 1935 Edward Said is born in Jerusalem; his book *Orientalism* (1978) helped to spur the development of postcolonial studies. "The Orient is watched, since its almost (but never quite) offensive behavior issues out of a reservoir of infinite peculiarity; the European, whose sensibility tours the Orient, is a watcher, never involved, always detached, always ready for new examples of what the Description de l'Egypte called 'bizarre jouissance.'"

NOVEMBER 4, 1780 Quechua leader Túpac Amaru II leads an indigenous rebellion against

TUESDAY NOVEMBER 02

Spanish control of Peru, beginning with the capture and killing of the Spanish governor by his slave. "There are no accomplices here but you and I. You the oppressor and I the liberator. Both of us deserve to die." —TÚPAC AMARU II, LAST WORDS TO GENERAL JOSÉ ANTONIO DE ARECHE

WEDNESDAY NOVEMBER 03

_____
_____
_____
_____
_____
_____
_____

Martin Luther (1529) by Lucas Cranach the Elder

THURSDAY NOVEMBER 04

_____
_____
_____
_____
_____
_____
_____

NOTES:

_____
_____
_____
_____
_____
_____

FRIDAY NOVEMBER 05

_____
_____
_____
_____
_____
_____
_____

SATURDAY NOVEMBER 06

_____
_____
_____
_____
_____
_____

SUNDAY NOVEMBER 07

_____

_____

_____

_____

_____

_____

MONDAY NOVEMBER 08

_____

_____

_____

_____

_____

_____

TUESDAY NOVEMBER 09

_____

_____

_____

_____

_____

_____

_____

NOVEMBER 7, 1917 Lenin leads the Bolsheviks in revolution against the provisional Russian government, establishing what will become the Soviet Union. "Freedom in capitalist society always remains about the same as it was in the ancient Greek republics: freedom for the slave-owners."
—THE STATE AND REVOLUTION

NOVEMBER 8, 1775 Thomas Spence, English radical and advocate for common ownership of land, delivers a speech with one of the earliest uses of the term "Rights of Man."

"Ye landlords vile, whose man's place mar,
Come levy rents here if you can;
Your stewards and lawyers I defy,
And live with all the RIGHTS OF MAN"

—"THE REAL RIGHTS OF MAN"

NOVEMBER 8, 1926 Antonio Gramsci, leader of the Italian Communist Party, is arrested by Mussolini and sentenced to twenty years in prison, during which time he would write his famous _Prison Notebooks_. "'Vanguards' without armies to back them up, 'commandos' without infantry or artillery, these too are transpositions from the language of rhetorical heroism." —"VOLUNTARISM AND SOCIAL MASSES"

NOVEMBER 10, 1995 Nigerian government hangs Ken Saro-Wiwa and the rest of the Ogoni Nine for their campaigning against the oil industry, and especially Royal Dutch Shell. "Dance your anger and your joys; dance the military guns to silence; dance their dumb laws to the dump; dance oppression and injustice to death; dance the end of Shell's ecological war of thirty years."
—STATEMENT OF THE OGONI PEOPLE TO THE TENTH SESSION OF THE WORKING GROUP IN INDIGENOUS POPULATIONS

WEDNESDAY NOVEMBER 10

_____

_____

_____

_____

_____

_____

_____

Lenin speaking at an assembly of Red Army troops bound for the Polish front, with Trotsky at the base, Moscow, 1920

THURSDAY NOVEMBER 11

_____

_____

_____

_____

_____

_____

NOTES:

_____

_____

_____

_____

_____

_____

FRIDAY NOVEMBER 12

_____

_____

_____

_____

_____

_____

SATURDAY NOVEMBER 13

_____

_____

_____

_____

_____

_____

SUNDAY NOVEMBER 14

_____

_____

_____

_____

_____

_____

_____

MONDAY NOVEMBER 15

_____

_____

_____

_____

_____

_____

TUESDAY NOVEMBER 16

_____

_____

_____

_____

_____

_____

_____

NOVEMBER 15, 1781 Túpac Katari, Aymara leader of an army that laid siege to the Spanish colonial city of La Paz, Bolivia, is betrayed and killed. "I die but will return tomorrow as thousand thousands." —KATARI'S LAST WORDS

NOVEMBER 15, 1988 Palestinian Declaration of Independence, written by poet Mahmoud Darwish, is proclaimed.

NOVEMBER 16, 1885 Louis Riel, Métis leader who headed two rebellions against a Canadian incursion into their territory, is hanged for treason. "I will perhaps be one day acknowledged as more than a leader of the half-breeds, and if I am I will have an opportunity of being acknowledged as a leader of good in this great country." —RIEL'S FINAL STATEMENT TO THE JURY

NOVEMBER 19, 1915 Joe Hill, militant songwriter and organizer with the International Workers of the World, is executed by firing squad. "Don't waste any time in mourning—organize." —HILL'S FAREWELL LETTER TO BILL HAYWOOD

NOVEMBER 19, 1979 Angela Davis—black feminist, philosopher, and prison abolitionist—wins the vice presidential nomination for the US Communist Party. "Prisons do not disappear problems, they disappear human beings. And the practice of disappearing vast numbers of people from poor, immigrant, and racially marginalized communities has literally become big business." —"MASKED RACISM"

NOVEMBER 20, 1969 The Native American group Indians of All Tribes occupies Alcatraz island in the San Francisco Bay and holds it for fourteen months. "Alcatraz Island is more than suitable as an Indian Reservation, as determined by the white man's own standards." —ALCATRAZ PROCLAMATION

WEDNESDAY NOVEMBER 17

Angela Davis on her first visit to the Soviet Union, 1972

THURSDAY NOVEMBER 18

NOTES:

FRIDAY NOVEMBER 19

SATURDAY NOVEMBER 20

SUNDAY NOVEMBER 21

MONDAY NOVEMBER 22

TUESDAY NOVEMBER 23

NOVEMBER 24, 1947 House Un-American Activities Committee votes to hold the "Hollywood Ten," a group of writers and directors blacklisted for their communist affiliations, in contempt of Congress. "We are men of peace, we are men who work and we want no quarrel. But if you destroy our peace, if you take away our work, if you try to range us one against the other, we will know what to do."
—*SPARTACUS* SCREENWRITER DALTON TRUMBO'S ANTIWAR NOVEL, *JOHNNY GOT HIS GUN*

NOVEMBER 24, 2014 A white police officer is acquitted in the shooting death of an unarmed black teenager, Michael Brown, in Ferguson, Missouri, setting off protests nationwide under the moniker Black Lives Matter.

NOVEMBER 25, 1832 Abd al-Qader al-Jaza'iri, Sufi and Muslim scholar and Algerian resistance leader, is elected emir of a confederation of tribes that banded together and fought the French invaders for over a decade. "If we leave them alone, they will assault us."

NOVEMBER 25, 1911 Mexican revolutionary Emiliano Zapata proclaims his Plan de Ayala, laying out his ideology and program of land reform, whose slogan "Land and Freedom!" was a watchword of the Mexican Revolution. "The nation is tired of false men and traitors who make promises like liberators and who on arriving in power forget them and constitute themselves as tyrants."

WEDNESDAY NOVEMBER 24

Black Lives Matter protest against police brutality, 2015

THURSDAY NOVEMBER 25

NOTES:

FRIDAY NOVEMBER 26

SATURDAY NOVEMBER 27

THE VERSO BOOK OF FEMINISM:
A SELECTION
EDITED BY JESSIE KINDIG

Proverb from the Cheyenne people

A nation is not conquered until
the hearts of its women
are on the ground.
Then it is done, no matter
how brave its warriors
nor how strong their weapons.

This proverb is from the native Tsétsêhéstâhese peoples of the Great Plains of North America, commonly known as the Cheyenne.

Moderata Fonte, "The Worth of Women," 1600

Do you really believe ... that everything historians tell us about men—or about women—is actually true? You ought to consider the fact that these histories have been written by men, who never tell the truth except by accident.

Born in Venice in 1555, Moderata Fonte built her reputation as a writer before marrying at twenty-seven. In The Worth of Women, *Fonte argued for women's superiority to men based on their intelligence. Fonte died in childbirth at thirty-seven; her tomb's epitaph declares Fonte "a very learned woman."*

Flora Tristan, "The Emancipation of Woman, or the Testament of the Pariah," 1843

The most oppressed man finds a being to oppress, his wife: she is the proletarian of the proletarian.

French–Peruvian socialist Flora Tristan, grandmother of Paul Gauguin, published her call for the self-emancipation of the working class, The Workers' Union, *one year before her death in 1844. She was among the first to argue that the liberation of women and the proletariat were mutual preconditions. This selection is taken from a collection of her writings and research notes published after her death.*

Bernadette Devlin McAliskey, "Campaign Slogan," 1968

I will take my seat and
fight for your rights.

In 1969, at the age of twenty-one, Irish Catholic Bernadette Devlin McAliskey was elected to Parliament to represent Northern Ireland. She took her seat with this memorable phrase, and devoted her career as a politician and activist to fighting for self-determination and freedom for Northern Ireland.

Swazi Wedding Song, "Song Seven," ca. 1990

I got married young.
I do not have any energy left.
All my energy got wasted in marriage.
All my energy, all my strength is gone,
    oh my Lord.
I got married young.
All my strength is gone.
Marriage has defeated me.
All my energy is gone.
Marriage has defeated me.

Recorded in the early 1990s in Swaziland, a series of communal Swazi wedding songs describes the ways women are expected to conform to often oppressive conditions of marriage.

Catrina Felton and Liz Flanagan, "A Tidda's Manifesto," 1993

The elevated status that White women have enables them to secure the resources to control feminism ... Generally speaking White feminists have not recognised or challenged the implications of racism or the historical and political discrimination that Koori women face ... That is why many Koori tiddas view feminism as simply another White politically controlled institution, established to benefit White women, first and foremost.

This manifesto from Australian Aboriginal "tiddas"—sisters—charges white Australian feminism with racism, a legacy of the country's settler colonial history.

These are revised extracts from The Verso Book of Feminism: Revolutionary Words from Four Millennia of Rebellion, *edited by Jessie Kindig (Verso, 2020).*

The BOOK of

FEMINISM

Edited by Jessie Kindig

Revolutionary Words from Four Millennia of Rebellion

SUNDAY NOVEMBER 28

NOVEMBER 29, 1947 The UN approves the partition of Palestine, despite its rejection by Palestinian Arabs and the fact that 90 percent of privately held land was Arab-owned.

"They've prohibited oppression among themselves
but for us they legalized all prohibitions!
They proclaim, 'Trading with slaves is unlawful'
but isn't the trading of free people more of a crime?"

—PALESTINIAN POET ABU SALMA, "MY COUNTRY ON PARTITION DAY"

MONDAY NOVEMBER 29

DECEMBER 1, 1955 Rosa Parks is arrested for refusing to give up her seat on a segregated bus, which triggers a boycott organized by the Women's Political Council of Montgomery. "Negroes have rights, too, for if Negroes did not ride the busses, they could not operate."
—WOMEN'S POLITICAL COUNCIL PAMPHLET

DECEMBER 2, 1964 Berkeley Free Speech Movement leader Mario Savio gives his famous speech on the steps of Sproul Hall. The next day, nearly 800 protesters are arrested on the UC Berkeley campus while resisting restrictions on political speech. "You've got to put your bodies upon the gears and upon the wheels ... upon the levers, upon all the apparatus, and you've got to make it stop."

TUESDAY NOVEMBER 30

DECEMBER 4, 1969 Fred Hampton, Black Panther leader, is assassinated in a raid on his apartment by the Chicago Police with the help of the FBI. "We've got to go up on the mountaintop to make this motherfucker understand, goddamnit, that we are coming from the valley!" —HAMPTON SPEECH AT OLIVET CHURCH

WEDNESDAY DECEMBER 01

Rosa Parks (1913–2005) being fingerprinted after her arrest for boycotting public transportation in Montgomery, Alabama, 1956

THURSDAY DECEMBER 02

NOTES:

FRIDAY DECEMBER 03

SATURDAY DECEMBER 04

SUNDAY DECEMBER 05

DECEMBER 5, 1978 Wei Jingsheng posts his manifesto "The Fifth Modernization," which was critical of the Communist leadership, to Beijing's Democracy Wall, and is imprisoned for 15 years. "Let us find out for ourselves what should be done."

DECEMBER 6, 1928 The United Fruit Company violently suppresses a workers' strike in Colombia, in what becomes known as the Banana Massacre.

DECEMBER 9, 2002 To Huu, one of the Viet Minh's most celebrated poets, dies.

"The ditches must go deeper than my hatred.
The work must fly faster than my tears."
—"GUERILLA WOMAN"

MONDAY DECEMBER 06

DECEMBER 10, 2008 Charter 08, a document for greater democratization, is published, signed by more than 350 Chinese writers, including poet and essayist Woeser, and human rights activist Liu Xiaobo. "The decline of the current system has reached the point where change is no longer optional."

DECEMBER 11, 1977 Moroccan poet Saida Menebhi dies in prison after a thirty-four-day hunger strike. Her work was central in the nationwide attempt to recover the history of the thousands of people who were "disappeared" in the 1970s and 1980s.

TUESDAY DECEMBER 07

"Prison is ugly
you draw it my child
with black marks
for the bars and grills"

DECEMBER 11, 2012 Theresa Spence, Chief of Attawapiskat First Nations in Canada, begins a hunger strike that would set off the indigenous sovereignty movement Idle No More.

WEDNESDAY DECEMBER 08

Protest in Hong Kong against the arrest of Liu Xiaobo, one of the authors of Charter 08

THURSDAY DECEMBER 09

NOTES:

FRIDAY DECEMBER 10

SATURDAY DECEMBER 11

SUNDAY DECEMBER 12

_____

_____

_____

_____

_____

_____

_____

MONDAY DECEMBER 13

_____

_____

_____

_____

_____

_____

_____

TUESDAY DECEMBER 14

_____

_____

_____

_____

_____

_____

_____

DECEMBER 13, 1797 Heinrich Heine, German-Jewish poet and essayist, is born. No writer would be more hated by the Nazis.

> "Ye fools, so closely to search my trunk!
> Ye will find in it really nothing:
> My contraband goods I carry about
> In my head, not hid in my clothing"
> —"A WINTER'S TALE"

DECEMBER 14, 2008 Iraqi journalist Muntadhar al-Zaidi throws his shoe at US president George W. Bush at a press conference. "This is a farewell kiss from the Iraqi people, you dog."

DECEMBER 16, 1656 Radical English Quaker leader James Nayler is arrested for blasphemy after reenacting Christ's entry into Jerusalem by entering Bristol on a donkey. "There is a spirit which I feel that delights to do no evil, nor to revenge any wrong, but delights to endure all things, in hope to enjoy its own in the end."
—NAYLER'S FINAL STATEMENT

DECEMBER 17, 1830 Simón Bolívar, nicknamed "El Libertador" for leading Bolivia, Colombia, Ecuador, Panama, Peru, and his native Venezuela to independence from Spain, dies. "If my death will help to end factions and to consolidate the Union, I shall go to my grave in peace." —A PROCLAMATION ISSUED A WEEK BEFORE HIS DEATH

DECEMBER 18, 2010 Demonstrations begin in Tunisia, the day after street vendor Mohammed Bouazizi self-immolated in protest of harassment from officials, setting off what would eventually become the Arab Spring.

WEDNESDAY DECEMBER 15

Muntadhar al-Zaidi is pulled away after throwing his shoes at George W. Bush

THURSDAY DECEMBER 16

NOTES:

FRIDAY DECEMBER 17

SATURDAY DECEMBER 18

SUNDAY DECEMBER 19

_____

_____

_____

_____

_____

_____

_____

MONDAY DECEMBER 20

_____

_____

_____

_____

_____

_____

_____

TUESDAY DECEMBER 21

_____

_____

_____

_____

_____

_____

_____

_____

DECEMBER 19, 1944 US soldier Kurt Vonnegut becomes a Nazi prisoner of war. The experience later shapes his novels, which often explore anti-authoritarian and anti-war themes. "There is no reason goodness cannot triumph over evil, so long as the angels are as organized as the Mafia." —CAT'S CRADLE

DECEMBER 23, 1986 Dissident and Nobel Peace Prize–winner Andrei Sakharov returns to Moscow after six years spent in internal exile for protesting the Soviet war in Afghanistan. "Freedom of thought is the only guarantee against an infection of people by mass myths, which, in the hands of treacherous hypocrites and demagogues, can be transformed into bloody dictatorship."

DECEMBER 25, 1831 Samuel Sharpe, leader of the Native Baptists of Montego Bay, leads Jamaican slaves in the Great Jamaican Slave Revolt, which was instrumental in abolishing chattel slavery. "I would rather die upon yonder gallows than live in slavery." —SHARPE'S LAST WORDS

DECEMBER 25, 1927 B. R. Ambedkar, an architect of the Indian constitution who was born into the Dalit caste of "untouchables," leads followers to burn the Manusmriti, an ancient text justifying the hierarchy. The "untouchables" were relegated to occupations considered impure, like butchering and waste removal.

DECEMBER 25, 1977 Domitila Barrios de Chungara, an activist with the militant Bolivian labor group Housewives' Committee, begins a hunger strike that leads to the end of the US-backed Bolivian dictatorship. "The first battle to be won is to let the woman, the man, the children participate in the struggle of the working class, so that the home can become a stronghold that the enemy can't overcome."

WEDNESDAY DECEMBER 22

B. R. Ambedkar during his tenure as chairman of the committee for drafting the constitution, 1950

THURSDAY DECEMBER 23

NOTES:

FRIDAY DECEMBER 24

SATURDAY DECEMBER 25

SUNDAY DECEMBER 26

_____

_____

_____

_____

_____

_____

_____

_____

MONDAY DECEMBER 27

_____

_____

_____

_____

_____

_____

_____

TUESDAY DECEMBER 28

_____

_____

_____

_____

_____

_____

_____

DECEMBER 30, 1884 William Morris, Eleanor Marx, and others establish the Socialist League, a revolutionary organization in the UK. "Civilization has reduced the workman to such a skinny and pitiful existence, that he scarcely knows how to frame a desire for any life much better." —MORRIS, "HOW I BECAME A SOCIALIST"

DECEMBER 30, 1896 José Rizal, Filipino nationalist revolutionary and writer, is executed by the Spanish on charges of rebellion, sedition, and conspiracy.

DECEMBER 31, 1977 Kenyan writer Ngũgĩ wa Thiong'o is imprisoned for cowriting a play critical of the Kenyan government.

> "We the workers in factories and plantations
>   said in one voice:
> We reject slave wages!
> Do you remember the 1948 general strike?"
> —NGŨGĨ WA THIONG'O AND NGŨGĨ WA MIRII, _I WILL MARRY WHEN I WANT_

DECEMBER 973 Philosopher and poet Abu Ala Al-Ma'arri, a constant champion of reason against superstition, authority and tradition, is born near Aleppo, Syria.

> "But some hope a divine leader with
>   prophetic voice
> Will rise amid the gazing silent ranks
> An idle thought! There's none to lead but
>   reason,
> To point the morning and evening ways."

JANUARY 1, 1970 Gil Scott-Heron, the poet and recording artist who became a voice of black protest culture, releases his album _Small Talk at 125th and Lenox_, whose opening track is, "The Revolution Will Not be Televised."

> "The revolution will not make you look five
>   pounds thinner,
> the revolution will not be televised, Brother."

WEDNESDAY DECEMBER 29

_____

_____

_____

_____

_____

_____

_____

Gil Scott-Heron (1949–2011)

THURSDAY DECEMBER 30

_____

_____

_____

_____

_____

_____

_____

NOTES:

_____

_____

_____

_____

_____

_____

FRIDAY DECEMBER 31

_____

_____

_____

_____

_____

_____

_____

SATURDAY JANUARY 01

_____

_____

_____

_____

_____

_____

V

VERSO READING LISTS

RADICAL HISTORIES

INSURGENT EMPIRE: ANTICOLONIALISM AND THE MAKING OF BRITISH DISSENT
PRIYAMVADA GOPAL

ONE MAN'S TERRORIST: A POLITICAL HISTORY OF THE IRA
DANIEL FINN

WE FIGHT FASCISTS: THE 43 GROUP AND THE FORGOTTEN BATTLE FOR POSTWAR BRITAIN
DANIEL SONABEND

A WORLD TO WIN: THE LIFE AND WORKS OF KARL MARX
SVEN-ERIC LIEDMAN

OCTOBER: THE STORY OF THE RUSSIAN REVOLUTION
CHINA MIÉVILLE

THE AMERICAN CRUCIBLE: SLAVERY, EMANCIPATION AND HUMAN RIGHTS
ROBIN BLACKBURN

LINEAGES OF THE ABSOLUTIST STATE
PERRY ANDERSON

ECOLOGY AND CLIMATE CHANGE

HOW TO BLOW UP A PIPELINE: LEARNING TO FIGHT IN A WORLD ON FIRE
ANDREAS MALM

THE CASE FOR THE GREEN NEW DEAL
ANN PETTIFOR

A PLANET TO WIN: WHY WE NEED A GREEN NEW DEAL
KATE ARONOFF, ALYSSA BATTISTONI, ET AL.

THE CLIMATE CRISIS AND THE GLOBAL GREEN NEW DEAL: THE POLITICAL ECONOMY OF SAVING THE PLANET
NOAM CHOMSKY AND ROBERT POLLIN

BEYOND BARBARISM: A MANIFESTO FOR A PLANET ON FIRE
MATTHEW LAWRENCE AND LAURIE LAYBOURN-LANGTON

FOSSIL CAPITAL: THE RISE OF STEAM POWER AND THE ROOTS OF GLOBAL WARMING
ANDREAS MALM

WORK AND AUTOMATION

INVENTING THE FUTURE: POSTCAPITALISM AND A WORLD WITHOUT WORK
NICK SRNICEK AND ALEX WILLIAMS

BREAKING THINGS AT WORK
GAVIN MUELLER

CLOCKING OFF: WHY WE NEED A SHORTER WORKING WEEK
KYLE LEWIS AND WILL STRONG

WHY YOU SHOULD BE A TRADE UNIONIST
LEN McCLUSKEY

FULLY AUTOMATED LUXURY COMMUNISM: A MANIFESTO
AARON BASTANI

FEMINISM AND GENDER

THE VERSO BOOK OF FEMINISM:
REVOLUTIONARY WORDS FROM FOUR
MILLENNIA OF REBELLION
EDITED BY JESSIE KINDIG

FULL SURROGACY NOW:
FEMINISM AGAINST FAMILY
SOPHIE LEWIS

FEMALES
ANDREA LONG CHU

FEMINISM FOR THE 99%: A MANIFESTO
CINZIA ARRUZZA, TITHI BHATTACHARYA AND
NANCY FRASER

BURN IT DOWN!
FEMINIST MANIFESTOS FOR THE REVOLUTION
EDITED BY BREANNE FAHS

REVOLTING PROSTITUTES:
THE FIGHT FOR SEX-WORKERS' RIGHTS
MOLLY SMITH AND JUNO MAC

FEMINISM AND NATIONALISM
IN THE THIRD WORLD
KUMARI JAYAWARDENA

ECONOMICS

THE NEW SPIRIT OF CAPITALISM
LUC BOLTANSKI AND EVE CHIAPELLO

THE PRODUCTION OF MONEY:
HOW TO BREAK THE POWER OF BANKERS
ANN PETTIFOR

THE COMPLETE WORKS OF ROSA LUXEMBURG,
VOLUME II: ECONOMIC WRITINGS 2
ROSA LUXEMBURG

A COMPANION TO MARX'S CAPITAL,
VOLUME 1 AND VOLUME 2
DAVID HARVEY

FORTUNES OF FEMINISM: FROM STATE-
MANAGED CAPITALISM TO NEOLIBERAL CRISIS
NANCY FRASER

RACE AND ETHNICITY

FUTURES OF BLACK RADICALISM
EDITED BY GAYE THERESA JOHNSON
AND ALEX LUBIN

MISTAKEN IDENTITY:
RACE AND CLASS IN THE AGE OF TRUMP
ASAD HAIDER

IF THEY COME IN THE MORNING … :
VOICES OF RESISTANCE
EDITED BY ANGELA Y. DAVIS

RACECRAFT: THE SOUL OF INEQUALITY
IN AMERICAN LIFE
KAREN E. FIELDS AND BARBARA J. FIELDS

HOW EUROPE UNDERDEVELOPED AFRICA
WALTER RODNEY

BEYOND BLACK AND WHITE:
FROM CIVIL RIGHTS TO BARACK OBAMA
MANNING MARABLE

ACTIVISM AND RESISTANCE

THE VERSO BOOK OF DISSENT:
REVOLUTIONARY WORDS FROM THREE
MILLENNIA OF REBELLION AND RESISTANCE
EDITED BY ANDREW HSIAO AND AUDREA LIM

POLICE: A FIELD GUIDE
DAVID CORREIA AND TYLER WALL

OUR HISTORY IS THE FUTURE:
STANDING ROCK VERSUS THE DAKOTA
ACCESS PIPELINE, AND THE LONG TRADITION
OF INDIGENOUS RESISTANCE
NICK ESTES

DIRECT ACTION: PROTEST AND THE
REINVENTION OF AMERICAN RADICALISM
L.A. KAUFFMAN

POLICING THE PLANET:
WHY THE POLICING CRISIS LED TO
BLACK LIVES MATTER
EDITED BY JORDAN T. CAMP AND
CHRISTINA HEATHERTON

ART AND AESTHETICS

**ARTIFICIAL HELLS: PARTICIPATORY ART
AND THE POLITICS OF SPECTATORSHIP**
CLAIRE BISHOP

SAVAGE MESSIAH
LAURA GRACE FORD

**ALL THAT IS SOLID MELTS INTO AIR:
THE EXPERIENCE OF MODERNITY**
MARSHALL BERMAN

PORTRAITS: JOHN BERGER ON ARTISTS
JOHN BERGER

**AISTHESIS: SCENES FROM
THE AESTHETIC REGIME OF ART**
JACQUES RANCIÈRE

CITIES AND ARCHITECTURE

**FEMINIST CITY:
CLAIMING SPACE IN A MAN-MADE WORLD**
LESLIE KERN

**MUNICIPAL DREAMS:
THE RISE AND FALL OF COUNCIL HOUSING**
JOHN BOUGHTON

**EXTRASTATECRAFT:
THE POWER OF INFASTRUCTURE SPACE**
KELLER EASTERLING

**CAPITAL CITY:
GENTRIFICATION AND THE REAL ESTATE STATE**
SAMUEL STEIN

**REBEL CITIES: FROM THE RIGHT TO THE CITY
TO THE URBAN REVOLUTION**
DAVID HARVEY

PHILOSOPHY AND THEORY

**THE FORCE OF NONVIOLENCE:
THE ETHICAL IN THE POLITICAL**
JUDITH BUTLER

**THE LEFT HEMISPHERE:
MAPPING CRITICAL THEORY TODAY**
RAZMIG KEUCHEYAN

CRITIQUE OF EVERYDAY LIFE
HENRI LEFEBVRE

**MINIMA MORALIA:
REFLECTIONS FROM DAMAGED LIFE**
THEODOR ADORNO

NO WALLS, NO BORDERS

**THE DISPOSSESSED: A STORY OF ASYLUM
AT THE US–MEXICAN BORDER AND BEYOND**
JOHN WASHINGTON

**HOSTILE ENVIRONMENT:
HOW IMMIGRANTS BECAME SCAPEGOATS**
MAYA GOODFELLOW

**ALL-AMERICAN NATIVISM: HOW THE BIPARTISAN WAR
ON IMMIGRANTS EXPLAINS POLITICS AS WE KNOW IT**
DANIEL DENVIR

**WE BUILT THE WALL:
HOW THE US KEEPS OUT ASYLUM SEEKERS FROM
MEXICO, CENTRAL AMERICA AND BEYOND**
EILEEN TRUAX

**VIOLENT BORDERS:
REFUGEES AND THE RIGHT TO MOVE**
REECE JONES

POLITICAL THEORY

**THE OLD IS DYING AND THE NEW CANNOT BE
BORN: FROM PROGRESSIVE NEOLIBERALISM
TO TRUMP AND BEYOND**
NANCY FRASER WITH BHASKAR SUNKARA

**HOW TO BE AN ANTICAPITALIST IN THE
TWENTY-FIRST CENTURY**
ERIK OLIN WRIGHT

**DEMOCRACY AGAINST CAPITALISM:
RENEWING HISTORICAL MATERIALISM**
ELLEN MEISKINS WOOD

**IMAGINED COMMUNITIES: REFLECTIONS ON
THE ORIGIN AND SPREAD OF NATIONALISM**
BENEDICT ANDERSON

FOR A LEFT POPULISM
CHANTAL MOUFFE